# ANTIQUE MAPS

of Europe, the Americas,
West Indies, Australasia,
Africa, the Orient

# ANTIQUE MAPS

of Europe, the Americas,
West Indies, Australasia,
Africa, the Orient

by DOUGLAS GOHM

OCTOPUS BOOKS

# Acknowledgements

The author and publisher
would like to express grateful
thanks to the following
individual and organizations
for all their help in supplying
original maps for photography:
Richard A. Nicholson, Bangor;
Parker Galleries, London;
Collectors' Treasures, Amersham.

Each map is credited to the above
using coding (N), (P) and (CT)

End papers: *Europe. Size of original 22½ × 34¼ ins. By A. H. Jaillot. Published in 1696.* (N)

Frontispiece: *The East Coast of North America. An interesting little chart engraved for Malham's* Naval Gazetteer. *Size of original 9⅜ × 7½ ins. Published 1801.* (CT)

Published by
OCTOPUS BOOKS
59 Grosvenor St
London W1

© Octopus Books Ltd 1972
ISBN 0 7064 0025 9
Filmset in Great Britain by
Keyspools Ltd, Golborne, Lancs

Cover design and
book layout by
Artes Graphicae Ltd
London

Produced by Mandarin Publishers Limited
77a Marble Road, North Point, Hong Kong
Printed in Hong Kong

# Contents

# Introduction

By definition a map is a graphic statement of direction and contour. It endeavours to represent three-dimensional surfaces on two-dimensional paper in such a way that a real appreciation of the terrain is conveyed to the reader of the map.

Modern cartographers have provided incredibly accurate maps of the world, moon and other celestial bodies, but to do this they all used advanced scientific techniques including aerial surveys. The early mapmakers, although endeavouring to make their work as accurate as possible, were limited to crude and inadequate equipment. During the fifteenth century when the earliest maps were produced, there was little background knowledge or reference sources available to the cartographer; in fact, during this period it was not possible to establish longitude with any real accuracy, neither was there an established unit of measurement. In England the mile of 1760 yards became statutory for London and Westminster in 1593, and with the expansion of the postal services in the seventeenth century it became the accepted unit for the post-mile throughout the kingdom. During 1824 the statutory mile was finally established by the Act for the Uniformity of Measures.

Fifteenth-century cartographers did not avail themselves of all the then known printing techniques, some of which involved the refinement of tonal graduations, but confined themselves to *relief* and *intaglio* blocks. Lithography made its debut during the nineteenth century, and whilst a number of collectors will consider this period too late for serious study, many interesting and attractive maps made their appearance.

The relief process was used mainly on woodblocks. A suitable block of wood of the appropriate size was prepared by making both surfaces smooth and flat. The map design was then drawn (in reverse) on the woodblock with ink, and with the aid of a knife, or graver, the engraver proceeded to cut away all the wood not marked in ink to a depth of about one-sixteenth of an inch or more, leaving the inked design standing proudly in relief.

To produce the actual map, a roller coated with ink was rubbed over the block so that only the raised design accepted a coating of ink. The paper was then laid on the block and rubbed manually on the back, or pressed, which transferred the image onto the paper. Later woodblocks were made by incising the design into the wood with a graver, but this technique was used mainly for picture illustrations.

The woods used generally for the blocks were pear, apple, lime and other soft woods; later boxwood in thicker sections superseded the softer types.

The intaglio process is the opposite of relief. The block in this process consisted of a sheet of copper, flat and thick enough to be rigid when taking impressions. The design was traced first on the copper; then, with a burin or graver, it was cut into the copper. By varying the pressure on the cutting tool the engraver was able to cut a groove of varying depth in the metal, which produced either a coarse or fine line on the finished impression.

From the mid-sixteenth century until 1820 copper was almost invariably the metal used, although very occasionally brass, zinc, iron and even silver were used. From 1820 steel, being a harder metal and in consequence more durable, slowly gained popularity over copper.

In the early fifteenth century and up to the middle of the sixteenth, the woodblock was the favoured means of producing maps. By the mid sixteenth century the cartographers of the Netherlands, already familiar with metal-working through the manufacture of mathematical instruments, turned to the intaglio or line-engraving process for the maps.

Decoration on early fifteenth-century maps was more or less restricted to the borders. The first half of the sixteenth century saw the ornamental cartouches, usually imitative of wood-carved scrolls, and the compass indicator, dividers, coats-of-arms, ships, cherubs, figures, and a host of other decorative devices.

The period from the mid-sixteenth century to the eighteenth is undoubtedly the one that interests collectors most. It was a period during which decorative cartography and technical achievement combined to produce maps of the finest quality.

Maps have been hand-coloured, to enhance them artistically and to embolden their engraved symbols, since the earliest days of their history. Many early map engravers were also skilled artists, and coloured their maps in the fashionable styles of manuscript cartography.

In the Netherlands artists already skilled in the art of illumination turned their attention to the colouring of maps, and by the middle of the sixteenth century map colouring had become a recognized trade. Map colourists worked either as independents, or as employees of map engravers. Not all maps were coloured, it was possible to purchase either 'coloured' or 'plain'. Today, maps with early or original colouring are generally more appreciated, and in consequence command higher prices.

As the decoration of Dutch and Flemish maps became more ornate, so the colouring became more elaborate also. Cartouches of tracery and strapwork were usually coloured in magenta or brown, with touches of gold, blue and other colours added for effect. Other embellishing features such as cherubs, fruits, figures, ribbons and monsters were coloured more or less realistically. Gold, often used in heraldic symbols, was represented by yellow; flesh tones by cochinal; the favourite colours for robes and garments were green shaded with a darker tint of the same colour, and vermilion shaded with carmine. Borders framing the maps were either yellow, light red or crimson. The hulls of ships were painted in umber; symbols representing towns or villages, red; hills, umber, sometimes shaded with green; trees and parklands were green, and the boundaries were washes of almost any colour, the rule being that

*'Anglia Regnum'. A beautiful antique coloured map of England and Wales by Jan Jansson, embellished with the Royal Coat-of-Arms, ships and a decorative cartouche. Size of original 15⅛ × 19½ ins. Published in Amsterdam in 1650. (CT)*

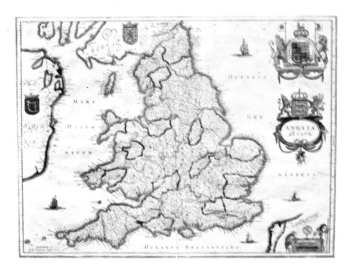

7

no two adjacent boundaries should be painted with the same colour. For rivers and lakes a thin wash of indigo was used.

Maps were, of course, printed in black on white paper and, to avoid continual reference for the heraldic colours, some engravers indicated the required tint by engraving small alphabetical letters in the spaces and quarters.

Other engravers used a method of shading and stippling to indicate the colours. A close look at a John Speed map, for instance, will reveal small alphabetical letters representing the initials of the colours, or tinctures, to use the heraldic term. This was the code:

O = Or, or gold, usually painted yellow (sometimes indicated by dots)

A = Argent or silver, left uncoloured (indicated by leaving plain)

G = Gules or red (indicated with vertical lines)

Az = Azure or blue (indicated with horizontal lines)

V = Vert or green (indicated with diagonal lines angled from left to right)

P = Purple (indicated by diagonal lines angled from right to left)

S = Sable or black (indicated with square cross-hatching, vertical and horizontal lines in close proximity forming tiny squares)

T = Tenne or tawny, usually painted in orange (indicated by diagonal cross-hatching).

Unfortunately there are many maps engraved with heraldic symbols and coats-of-arms that do not have these colours indicated by either method, which means that modern colourists of old un-coloured maps have to research the information, and if this becomes too tedious, there is a risk of colours being added for effect, rather than for accuracy.

Ptolemy's *Geographia*, produced in Alexandria about AD 160, referred to methods of mapmaking, but it was not until the fifteenth century that map-making as such developed, and although primarily concerned with assisting the traveller and recording land parcels, it must be assumed that, even in the fifteenth century, maps were appreciated as works of art just as much as for any scientific merit.

Early cartographers, like any other section of the community, had to earn a living, either by direct selling, as an employee, or by being patronized. Therefore, market requirements must have influenced the finished product, especially during a period when there was a natural tendency to combine the functional with the artistic.

Although there are antique maps covering the entire surface of the world, they were nearly all of European origin. The Dutch, Italian, German,

*'North America.' This map, by A. Findlay, gives prominence to natural features, lakes, rivers, headlands, etc. Size of original 10 × 7¾ ins. Published by Thomas Kelly for Barclay's* Dictionary of the United States *c 1840.* (CT)

NORTH AMERICA.

French and English were the predominant map-makers of the world from the fifteenth to the eighteenth century.

The following names are part of the history of cartography. Many of the examples in circulation today originated in their workshops, and any book on antique maps would be incomplete without reference to the craftsmen engravers and cartographers of yesterday.

A point worth noting in respect of dates shown on maps: these usually refer to the *original* issue, but as maps were often printed for years after without any alterations being made to the plate, the actual date of issue of a particular map can be much later than the date indicated on it.

*'Daniae Regnum.' An antique map by Matthäus Seutter of the Kingdom of Denmark and the Duchies of Schleswig and Holstein. Size of original 19½ × 22⅞ ins. Published in 1730.* (CT)

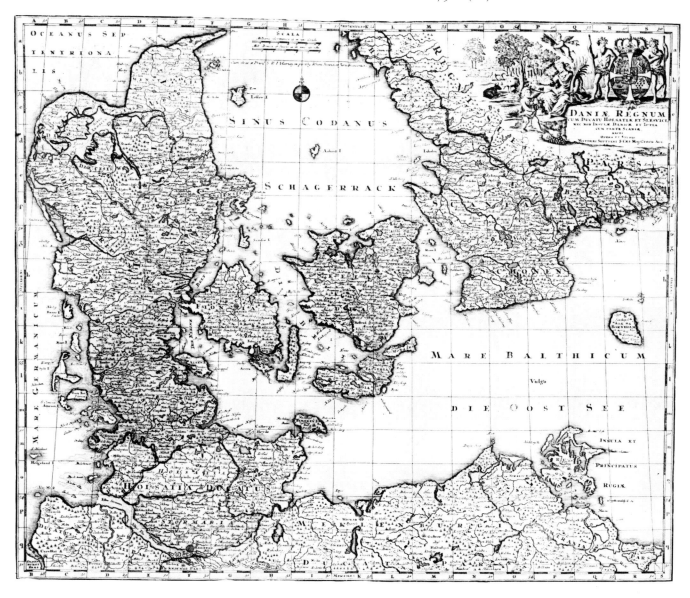

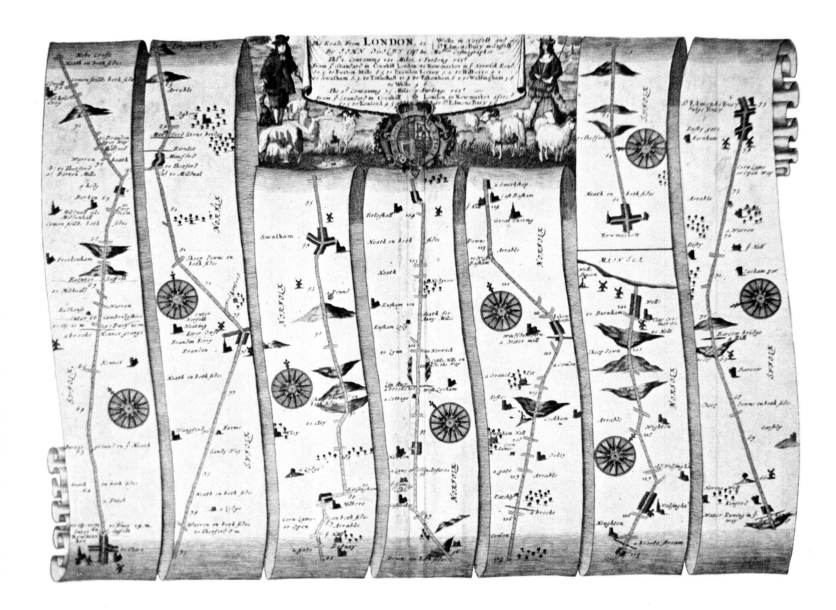

# THE
# MAPMAKERS

## Sebastian Münster (1489–1552)

Born in Hessen in 1489, and educated in both Tübingen and
Heidelberg, Sebastian Münster's earliest maps, produced from
from woodcuts, date from about 1530. He produced both
large and small maps including continental maps of Africa,
the Americas, and World maps.

In 1528 Münster requested German geographers to survey their
own provinces, and to forward the results of their work to him.
Of those received many were printed, together with
acknowledgements, in his *Cosmographia*, published initially
in Basel in 1550; in all there were some thirty editions,
terminating in 1628.

The Münster edition of Ptolemy was published in 1540.
He also produced a number of town views, usually bird's-eye
vistas executed in great detail, in which particular features
of houses, bridges, etc., were accurately noted.

## Gerard Mercator (1512–94)

Born in Rupelmonde, near Antwerp, in 1512,
Gerard Mercator was not only a cartographer of outstanding
ability, he was also a skilled engraver.

Until 1552 Mercator was a maker of mathematical and
astronomical instruments. It was during this period of his career
that he produced a number of splendid globes. His first map,
engraved on a copper plate, was published in 1537.

Nearly all his maps were original productions, being both
drawn and engraved by him.

Mercator produced an atlas issued in three parts, which was
published between the years 1585 and 1595. He also produced
maps of single countries and groups of countries.

After Mercator's death, his sons and grandsons continued to
issue his maps, supplemented with works of their own,
until 1606, when the plates were acquired by Jodocus Hondius,
who continued to issue maps from them.

# Abraham Ortelius (1527–98)

Born in Antwerp in 1527, Abraham Ortelius was a cartographer, illuminator and mapseller. A man of considerable education, he entered the business world in partnership with his sister, selling and colouring maps.

In 1570, he published the *Theatrum orbis Terrarum*, which can be considered the first 'modern' atlas designed with the emphasis on good cartography rather than appeal to the potential customer. The *Theatrum* was a fine collection of exquisite maps, which were subsequently reissued until about 1612. The text on the back was printed in Dutch, French, German, Latin, Spanish and finally, in 1606, in English. Ortelius was not an original worker: in fact, only five maps were known to have been made by him before 1570. In 1603, no less than 183 names of cartographers appeared in his 'Catalogue of Authors', prefixed to that year's edition of the atlas. Up to the time he produced his atlas, he sold maps published at his own expense direct to customers. His material thereafter was obtained by agents in foreign cities, from which his own engravers copied. Oertlius also produced a series of fine quality miniature maps from 1576.

# John Norden (1548–1626)

Born in 1548, probably in Somerset, England, John Norden set out to produce county maps from his own surveys, but after completing only a few he ran out of funds, and he was forced to discontinue the project. Norden's intention was to correct deficiencies he had observed in maps by Saxton and Camden, concerning roads, boundaries of the hundreds, reference grids, historical sites and so on.

However, the few surveys made by Norden were not entirely wasted. They resulted in maps of Middlesex (1953), Surrey (1954), Sussex, Hampshire (both 1595) and Hertfordshire (1598). Original copies of these maps are now rare, in fact only one copy of the Sussex map is known to exist, and that is in the library of the Royal Geographical Society.

Another Norden enterprise were his county handbooks entitled *Speculum Britanniae*; these were produced at his own expense – which may explain why only two volumes were brought out during his lifetime.

# John Speed (1552–1629)

John Speed was born in Cheshire, England, in 1552.
His early days were spent as a tailor, the profession of his father.
In 1580 he entered the Merchant Taylors' Company,
and married two years later.
Speed was also an antiquary and gained a reputation in the field
of history. He designed his *Theatre of the Empire of Great Britaine*
as a geographical prologue to an historical work for which he
had started to collect material about 1596. The *Theatre* was the
first printed atlas of the British Isles.
The *Theatre* followed the pattern of the Ortelius atlas,
with added decorative features designed to make it more of a
commercial success. Incidentally, the publishers John Sudbury
and George Humble must have had considerable confidence in
Speed to have invented in such an ambitious work. It is
interesting also to note that all the plates were engraved by
Jodocus Hondius in Amsterdam.
Speed was not an originator, he used the earlier works of other
cartographers as a reference source and made full use of the
work of Saxton and Norden. The backs of Speed's county maps
carry a description and history of the county on one half, and a
list of important towns and villages on the other. His early
maps were published in 1611–2 and were issued and reissued
many times, well into the eighteenth century.

# Christopher Saxton (*c* 1542–1606)

Christopher Saxton, an English cartographer, was born near Leeds in Yorkshire. He was educated at Cambridge and later went to London.

In 1575, the Privy Council issued a directive that Saxton should be 'assisted in all places necessary for him to survey certain counties'. This meant that authority was vested in him to gain access to property, climb privately owned hills, towers, etc. Thomas Seckford, an official of the Queen's court, obtained this authority for Saxton, and also supplied the necessary financial backing. The result of Saxton's surveys were committed to the engravers between 1574–9. As the technique of engraving on copper was far more advanced in the Netherlands, Flemish and Dutch craftsmen were employed and actually worked on fourteen of the plates – though all thirty-six show Dutch influence in their style of lettering and decoration. Remegius Hogenburg and Leonard Terwoort were two of the Dutch engravers employed; another craftsman, Augustine Ryther, although English, produced maps almost indistinguishable from those produced by the Dutch.

In 1557, Saxton received a ten-year privilege to engrave, print and sell maps, and it is likely that many maps produced during this period were obtainable in single sheets. In 1579 they were issued as an atlas with a frontispiece showing Queen Elizabeth as the patron of geography and astronomy. Saxton's maps were frequently reprinted to supply a popular market, and they continued in popularity until the arrival of Speed's county atlas, which took over that market. However, reworked and corrected plates of Saxton's maps were still being used as late as 1795.

## Pieter van den Keere (1571–*c* 1646)

Pieter van den Keere, a Dutch engraver, worked between about 1590 and 1620. He was also an artist of some merit and a bookseller. He spent much of his working life in England, and is thought to have worked with Jodocus Hondius. Sometime around 1599 van der Keere produced a 'pocket edition' of an atlas, using Saxton's maps as his basis. At that time the project seemed doomed to failure, but by 1627 the plates had been acquired by Speed's publishers, John Sudbury and George Humble, and from then onwards they became a very successful series.

One of van den Keere's most interesting engraved maps was produced in *Germanina Inferior* (Amsterdam, 1617): it is entitled 'The Seventeen Provinces' (of the United Netherlands) and is a very decorative map with figures and an outline boundary in the shape of a lion.

## Willem Jansz Blaeu (1571–*c* 1646)

A Dutch engraver, Willem Blaeu, was born in Amsterdam in 1571 and later died there. He had two sons, Joan Willem (1596–1673) and Cornelius, who died in 1642. This family was responsible for producing some of the finest maps of their period; the quality of their engraving, sense of design and beautiful cartouches have rarely, if ever, been surpassed. They produced a series of English county maps after Speed, and although they used the same basic information, including the heraldry, they recomposed presentation to give an entirely different map.

Willem Blaeu was by about 1596 in business as an instrument maker and globe manufacturer. In every aspect of his career Blaeu showed himself to be a fine technician. Later, when he became an engraver and printer, he invented an improved printing press. In 1633 his service to navigation was rewarded by his appointment as map-maker to the Republic. The Blaeu family also produced the earliest maps of the Scottish counties and provinces, engraved from surveys taken by Timothy Pont in the latter part of the sixteenth century.

## Nicolaes Visscher (1587–1637)

Claes (Nicolaes) Jansz Visscher was born in Amsterdam.
He worked initially for Hondius but subsequently set up his
own map-printing business. In due course the business passed
to his son, in 1637, and subsequently to his grandson in 1679.
They all bore the same name, but the son sometimes used a
Latinized version of his name, 'N. J. Piscator'. The son produced
large wall maps in the style of Blaeu and published his first atlas
in 1666. The son lived from 1618–79, the grandson, 1639–1709.

## Jan Jansson (1596–1664)

Jan Jansson was born in Arnhem in 1596 and died in
Amsterdam in 1664. He produced fine quality maps of English
and Welsh counties closely resembling the maps of Blaeu.
These were published between 1638–50 in various editions,
and republished later (c 1683) by Valk and Schenk.
When Jansson died, his business continued until 1694 under
the administration of his two sons-in-law, using the name
Janssonius-Waesbergh; the plates were then sold by auction.

## William Kip (fl 1598–1635)

William Kip was an English engraver. He worked between
1598 and 1635 approximately, and although his work was very
good, it lacked the quality of Jansson, Speed and Blaeu.
Kip, working with William Hole, produced a fine set of maps
of the English and Welsh counties. These were first issued in
1607 with Latin text on the back; they were reissued in 1610
without text on the back, and again in 1637 with a plain back
and a numeral engraved on the lower left-hand corner of the
majority of the counties.

## Nicolas Sanson (1600–67)

A French mapmaker of some reputation, Sanson was born in
Abbeville and died in Paris. He produced some very attractive
maps with decorative cartouches.
Sanson's maps were first gathered into atlas format from about
1645. They were very elegant and typically French in character,
and in consequence were later copied by Dutch, German and
English cartographers until well into the eighteenth century.
Sanson's engravers were either Flemish or from Picardy.

# John Ogilby (1600–76)

John Ogilby was born in Edinburgh. Although a man of many parts, his name immediately brings to mind his most famous achievement – his strip road maps.

These were a series of maps showing roads between large towns and were presented in the form of a continuous scroll. Hills and landmarks were noted to aid the traveller. The maps have a central cartouche, beautifully decorated, along the top margin giving details of the route. Each strip has a compass to indicate direction, and where a direction changes a second compass is added, and a dividing line drawn across the strip. These maps were the first to use the standard mile; until that time the length of a mile varied in different parts of the country, hence it is not unusual to find more than one scale on old maps.

Smaller copies of Ogilby's road maps were made by Thomas Gardner and John Senex. Ogiliby also produced a number of books dealing with the Americas, Asia and Africa.

# William Hole (*fl* 1607–46)

Little is known about the life of this English cartographer, except that he worked in London during most of the first half of the seventeenth century. He engraved the unusual maps used to illustrate Michael Drayton's poem 'Polyolbion' issued in 1612 and 1622, and he is also reputed to have been the first engraver to commit music to the copper plate.

However, it is mainly for his work in connection with county maps that he is known, a number of these being produced in conjunction with William Kip. As a basis for their map design they used Norden's and Saxton's surveys; the result was some fine, original work.

# Michael Drayton (1563–1631)

Michael Drayton, an Englishman, was not in a strict sense a cartographer: he was in reality a poet, but his 'Polyolbion', a long description of the geography and lore of Britain published in two parts in 1612 and 1622, did contain some maps of a kind. Very few places are named but important towns are marked by crowned figures; hills and mountains are shown more or less conventionally – though they are often capped with a seated shepherd; rivers contain nude nymphs, and some counties are grouped. The maps were engraved by William Hole and have a decorative value.

# Frederik de Wit the Elder (1616–98)

The maps of Frederik de Wit were typical of the style of his period, being competently executed and decorated with cartouches. The style of this Dutch cartographer was similar to Jansson and others, and many of his maps were reissues of Jansson. During the business life of the de Wits (he had a son of the same name) the plates were acquired of the 'townbooks' originally owned by Jansson, and the surviving plates of Joan Blaeu after his printing house was destroyed by fire in 1672. De Wit's son died in 1706, and the total stock of his plates was acquired by Pieter Mortier.

# Marco Vincenzo Coronelli (1650–1718)

Marco Vincenzo Coronelli was the most famous Italian cartographer of his period. In recognition of his work he received the appointment of Cosmographer to the Republic of Venice. He produced a series of large maps between 1690–7, the majority of which were decorated, and numerous other maps during his lifetime.

# Robert Morden (died 1703)

Robert Morden was an English bookseller, publisher and map-maker. His premises from 1688 to 1703 were in Cornhill, in the City of London.

His best known maps are those of English counties first published in 1695, and subsequently reissued in 1722, 1753 and 1772. These maps were nicely engraved with a moderately decorated cartouche and endowed with numerous place names. The first issue, of 1695, was in most cases printed with a good impression on rather thin paper; the second (1722) had a watermark of a horse encompassed in a circle, and was produced on somewhat thicker paper, the third and fourth (1753 and 1772) were printed on good quality, smoother paper.

Morden also produced maps of various parts of the world. These were often quite small and were issued from 1688.

He also originated a small set of county maps, issued initially in 1701. These are attractive little collector's items, and are rarer than the larger county maps.

## Sir William Petty (1623–c 1690)

Born in 1623 in Hampshire, England, William Petty was a man of science. He was a mathematician and was also sufficiently skilled in medicine to become Physician General to the Army then established in Ireland.

Whilst in Ireland, and encouraged by Cromwell's Government, he undertook a survey of the country. The quality of his work left much to be desired from an artistic standpoint, being somewhat crude and lacking the precision of line usually associated with antique maps. These maps were published in 1685, and they are now scarce. They were reissued in 1690 and again at an unknown date around the mid-nineteenth century. Various issues of a miniature set were published between 1685 and 1728.

## Johannes van Keulen (1654–1704)

Johannes van Keulen, a Dutch cartographer, is best known for the many fine sea charts contained in his *Zee-Atlas*, published in Amsterdam in 1681; an English edition was brought out one year later. In the charts the coast lines were strongly engraved with a double line and the cartouches were large and very ornate, and more often than not contained figures.

## Johann Baptists Homann (1664–1724)

J. B. Homann, a native of Nuremberg, started his career as a map engraver, but in 1702 he set up his own publishing house. The operation was an undoubted commercial success. Homann built up stocks of atlas plates and sold his maps at lower prices than the French and Dutch, who until then had dominated the market. (It is interesting to note that many of Homann's maps were copied from the French and Dutch.)

During the seventeenth century the German map trade was mainly dependent on the Dutch. There were, of course, German cartographers, but the industry could not compare favourably in terms either of output, quality or, even more important, in price with maps produced in Holland.

Homann, with his own workshops and business acumen, put the German map industry back in business, as it were, and in 1715 he was rewarded for his services by being appointed Geographer to the Emperor.

Homann's successors were J. C. Homann (1703–30) and J. M. Franz (1700–61); they adopted the imprint 'Homan'sche Erben'.

## John Seller (*fl* 1669–*c* 1700)

John Seller, an English mapmaker, produced numerous maps and
sea charts covering the major parts of the world. His best
known item is probably his *English Pilot*, but he also produced
sea charts covering the coasts of most parts of the world.
Many of his sea charts were printed from plates
acquired from the Dutch.
In 1695, he issued a set of miniature county maps,
which were reprinted in 1701. These continued to be issued
with minor alterations into the early nineteenth century.
Seller was one of the most prominent map sellers of the
seventeenth century. Apart from his cartographic activities,
he was also a maker of mathematical instruments to
Charles II and James II.

## Guillaume Delisle (1675–1726)

The maps of Guillaume Delisle were usually of very good quality.
Probably he is best known for his work in connection with the
recharting of the world map, correcting the previous concepts
which contained many longitude errors. He executed this work
in collaboration with his father, Claude Delisle and J. B.
Bourguignon d'Anville. Delisles maps were published from about
1700, his *Atlas Nouveau* incorporated the latest information
supplied by geodesists and astronomers.

## Matthäus Seutter (1678–1757)

Born in Angsberg, Seutter was a maker of scientific instruments,
and a publisher of maps. He made both celestial and terrestrial
globes, and eventually became Imperial Geographer to the
Emperor Charles VI. He was apprenticed in 1697 to John Baptist
Homann of Nurnberg, and his maps reflect the Homann influence
with their heavy black engraving and large ornate cartouches
abounding in flora, figures, fauna and other decorative devices.

## The younger Seutter (1729–60)

Examples of Seutters' more interesting maps are *Africa juxta
navigationes et observationes recentissmæ*. Pub. *c* 1740 Augsburg.
*Grosser atlas*, pub. *c* 1734 Augsburg. *Recens edita totius Novi
Belgii*. Pub. *c* 1735 Augsburg.

## John Adair (*fl* 1703)

John Adair's contribution to cartography was comparatively insignificant. In 1703 he produced a set of six sea charts of the Scottish coasts, but otherwise managed little of any great consequence.

## Richard Blome (died 1705)

He produced a set of county maps in 1673 decorated with cartouches and coats-of-arms, and he also issued a miniature series in 1671 and another in 1681; these were reprinted in various forms until about 1735. During the last years of the seventeenth century Blome also published maps of various parts of the world.

The maps of the English cartographer Richard Blome are, in the quality of the engraving, well below the standard of most antique maps. Blome was not a skilled craftsman and his maps lack the careful discipline usually found in such an exacting art. Nevertheless, they have some artistic merit and the fact that they also have antiquity makes them worthy of a place in the collector's folio.

## Herman Moll (died 1732)

A Dutchman by birth, Herman Moll came to England in the 1680s and set up in London as a bookseller and an engraver of maps. Initially he had premises in Blackfriars and later he was in the Strand. He produced a wide range of maps from miniature to very large, decorated with inset plans and pictures.

Moll's medium-sized county maps were engraved in thick black lines that became a hallmark of his particular style; interest heightened by illustrated features showing antiquities excavated in the county, such as coins, etc., or views. His Wiltshire map (1724) measures about $7\frac{1}{2} \times 12\frac{1}{2}$ ins and has two small views of Stonehenge in the top margins, and various excavated items on the lower margin. In addition to county maps, Moll also produced large ones of the World, India, North America, Scotland, and many others. He died in London.

## Captain Grenville Collins (1693–1785)

Grenville Collins was born in England in 1693. He surveyed the coastlines of the British Isles and produced charts that were both useful and decorative. The cartouches of Collins are usually the most dominant features of his charts; they are well designed and intricate and, when expertly coloured, are very beautiful indeed. Their first date of publication was in 1693, but they were reissued often during the eighteenth century.

# Jean-Baptiste d'Anville (1697–1782)

Jean-Baptiste Bourguignon d'Anville, to give him his full name, was born in 1697. This famous French mapmaker produced his maps during the period when a more scientific approach was being given to the subject, and consequently greater attention was paid to detail. In his work, although the quality of the geographical information was reformed, the cartouche remained decorative. D'Anville's well-known *Nouvel Atlas de la Chine* (The Hague, 1737) was prepared by him from surveys made by Jesuit missionaries who surveyed China for the Emperor between 1708–16. He was also responsible for a number of other maps. Other cartographers frequently copied his work.

# Edward Wells (*fl* 1700)

Edward Wells issued a set of maps at around the beginning of the eighteenth century. They were interesting examples of decorative cartography, and covered various parts of the world. Though not very valuable in terms of geography, they were strongly engraved and carried a decorative cartouche and a dedication to the Duke of Gloucester, together with his coat-of-arms.

# John Senex (*fl* 1700–40)

John Senex, an Englishman, worked in London.
Operating initially from premises in Cornhill, he later moved to the Globe, Salisbury Court, off Fleet Street.
In 1728 he produced a set of uninspired charts, sometimes with more than one map to a sheet. The engraving was executed by Senex and published in conjunction with Henry Wilson and John Harris.
However, the maps of Senex were considerably more interesting. In 1719 he issued a handy-sized road book, with small strip maps after Ogilby, but without decoration. He also engraved a set of large maps of various parts of the world.

# John Rocque (1704–62)

John Rocque flourished between about 1734 and 1762.
A Hugeunot, he spent the best years of his life working in London. He is probably recognized mainly for his survey of London, produced to a large scale and engraved by Pine and issued in 1746. He also produced a set of county maps, in which the county boundaries were shown by cross-hatching.

# Emanuel Bowen (*fl* 1700–67)

Emanuel Bowen was an English engraver and map seller who
had a place of business in Fleet Street, London. His output was
prodigious. He produced in about 1758 a series of small county
maps for W. Owen's *General Magazine of Arts and Sciences*.
These were boldly produced with a scroll design cartouche,
and the hundreds indicated. (A hundred is a subdivision of a
county, having its own court.)
Bowen also produced a large series of county maps in
conjunction with Thomas Kitchen. These were published from
1749–55, and a series of medium-sized maps followed in 1762,
most of which were endorsed with information in the blank
areas that described towns, products, climate, etc. Again it was
Bowen who was responsible for the beautiful *Britannia Depicta*,
based on Ogilby's road maps but with historical facts added,
also coats-of-arms and other heraldic information.
In addition to those already mentioned, Emanuel Bowen
issued and reissued numerous other maps, and after him the
business was continued by his son Thomas until shortly
before the latter died, in the workhouse, in 1790.

# Thomas Kitchen (1718–84)

Thomas Kitchen flourished in London between 1738–76.
He produced county maps and some of various parts of the
world. He is probably best known for his quarto-sized
county maps published in 1764.
The quality of Kitchen's engraving was excellent;
he was also an author, publisher and purveyor of artists'
materials which he sold from a shop in Holborn Hill.

# George Bickham (*fl* 1743)

George Bickham was an English engraver and author.
He was born in 1684 and flourished at Covent Garden, London.
His only work connected with maps were his strange bird's-eye
views of counties, first published *c* 1743.

## John Ellis (*fl* 1750–96)

John Ellis, an Englishman, was not a cartographer in the true sense, but rather a skilled engraver who included map engravings among his general activities. He produced a set of English county maps in 1766, using the quarto maps of Thomas Kitchen as a basis, but omitting the Kitchen cartouche and substituting a miniature scene.

## John Cary (*c* 1754–1835)

Although the appeal of antique maps comes mainly from the artistry of their decoration, the plainer maps of the later periods are nevertheless interesting to serious collectors.

John Cary's maps were utilitarian but they were beautifully engraved and accurately lettered.

John Cary, an Englishman, was born about 1754 and died in 1835; his engraving career started in the 1770s. He produced a great number of maps including two sets of county maps published in 1789 and 1805 and quarto-size county maps from 1793. His premises were initially in the Strand, London but later he removed to St James's Street.

## Thomas Jefferys (died 1771)

Thomas Jefferys flourished approximately during the same period as Kitchen: in fact, he engraved a set of small English county maps with Kitchen that were first issued in 1749. He also produced maps of various parts of the world, including the West Indies and North America.

## Thomas Moule (1784–1851)

Thomas Moule's English county maps, published in 1836, were highly decorated but have a 'modern' sense of cartography. They are covered with inset views, foliage, shields, etc., but it is unlikely that they will appeal to a serious collector. Moule was born in 1784 and died in 1851; he was a man of considerable talents, being, in addition, a noted authority on heraldry and antiquities.

26

# THE
# MAPS

*'Western Hemisphere, or New World'*
*and 'Eastern Hemisphere, or Old World'.*
*Size of original 8 × 16 ins. approx.*
*Published* c *1807 by J. Wilkes.* (CT)

*'Western Hemisphere.' A map with highly*
*decorative borders of Indians, Animals and*
*whales. Map drawn and engraved by J. Rapkin.*
*Illustrations by H. Warren, engraved by*
*J. Rogers. Published by J. & F. Tallis* c *1850.* (CT)

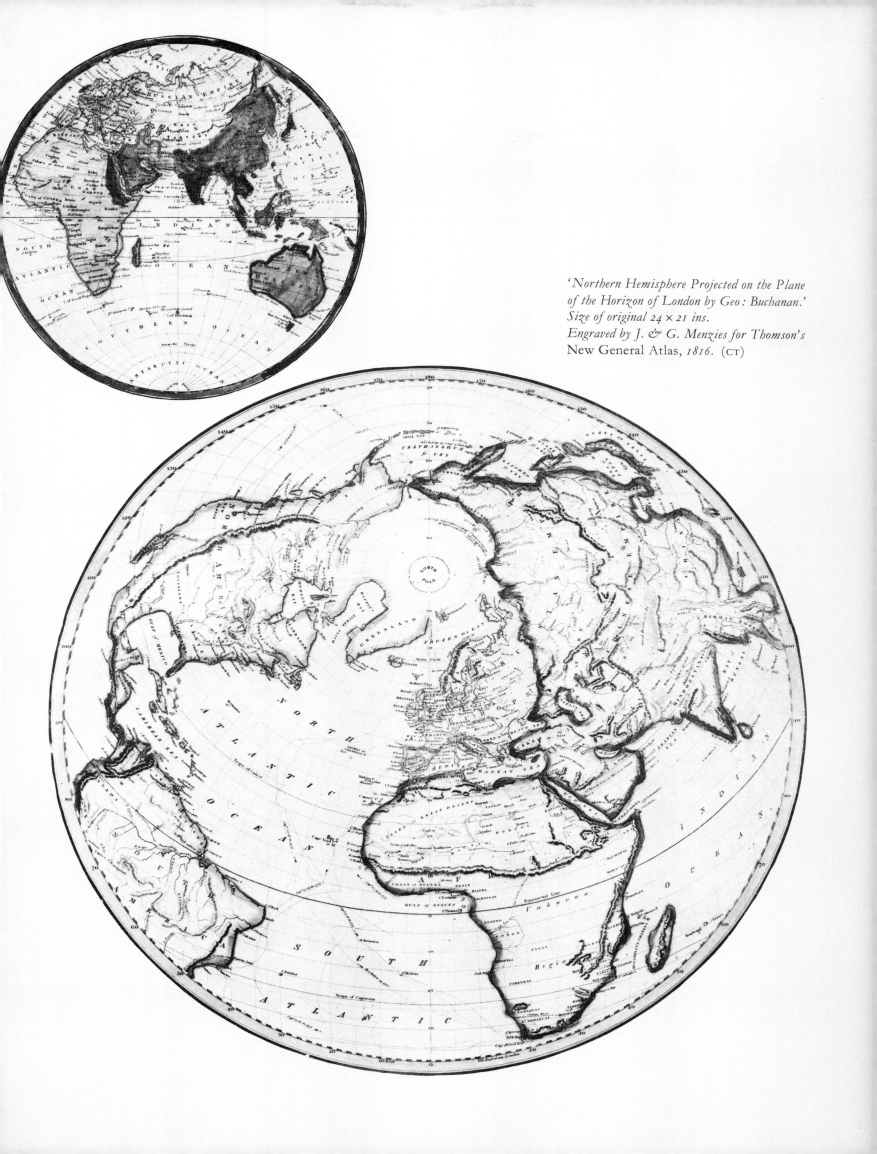

'Northern Hemisphere Projected on the Plane
of the Horizon of London by Geo: Buchanan.'
Size of original 24 × 21 ins.
Engraved by J. & G. Menzies for Thomson's
New General Atlas, 1816. (CT)

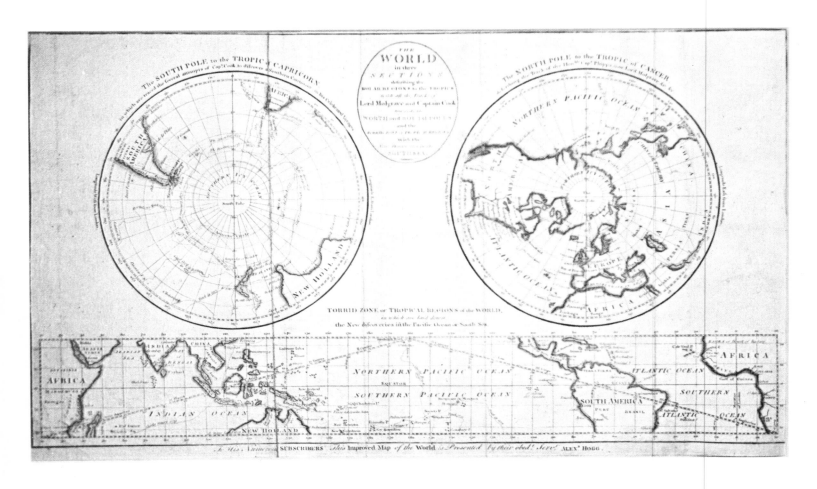

Miniature map of the World. Only 3¼ ins.
in diameter, this map is extremely rare, and .
only two copies are known to exist; one is
owned by S. Isler of Amersham, Bucks, the
other copy is in the possession of the British
Museum, London. It was engraved by W. Kip
in 1602, and most of the inscriptions are in
Latin, except the name 'Jehova', which is in
Hebrew. Inscribed on the bottom of the map are
the words 'Terra Australis Incognita', meaning
'the unknown land of the south'. The first verse
of Psalm 24, quoted in Latin, exclaims:
'The earth is the Lord's, and the fulness
thereof; the World and they that dwell therein'.
It is interesting to note the 'hand of God', the
forearm encircled by a collar of cool cloud
appearing out of a blazing sun and holding a
cord attached to the 'roof' of the world and,
as it were, pulling the world into the shape of a
spheroid to fit into the outer ring. (CT)

'The World.' A world map in three parts describing 'the Polar Regions to the Tropics with all the Tracks of Lord Mulgrave and Captain Cook'. Size of original 9¾ × 16½ ins.

Celestial Map. A star chart for the Northern Hemisphere by J. B. Homann, including a portion of the ecliptic (black-and-white line) with, around it from right to left, the zodiacal constellations Pisces, Aries, Taurus, Germini, Cancer, Leo and Virgo. Size of original 19 × 22½ ins. Published c 1730. (N)

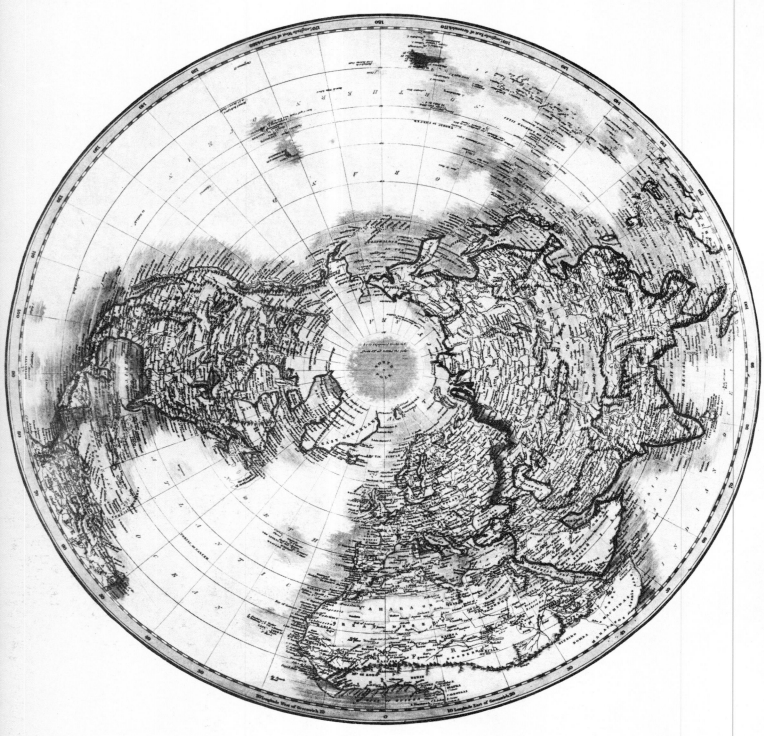

*'Northern Hemisphere.' Map engraved by Kirkwood for John Thomson. Size of original 24 × 21 ins. Published in 1814.* (CT)

*Celestial Chart. A Star chart by J. B. Homann calculated for the year 1730. Size of original 19½ × 23 ins. Published c 1720.* (N)

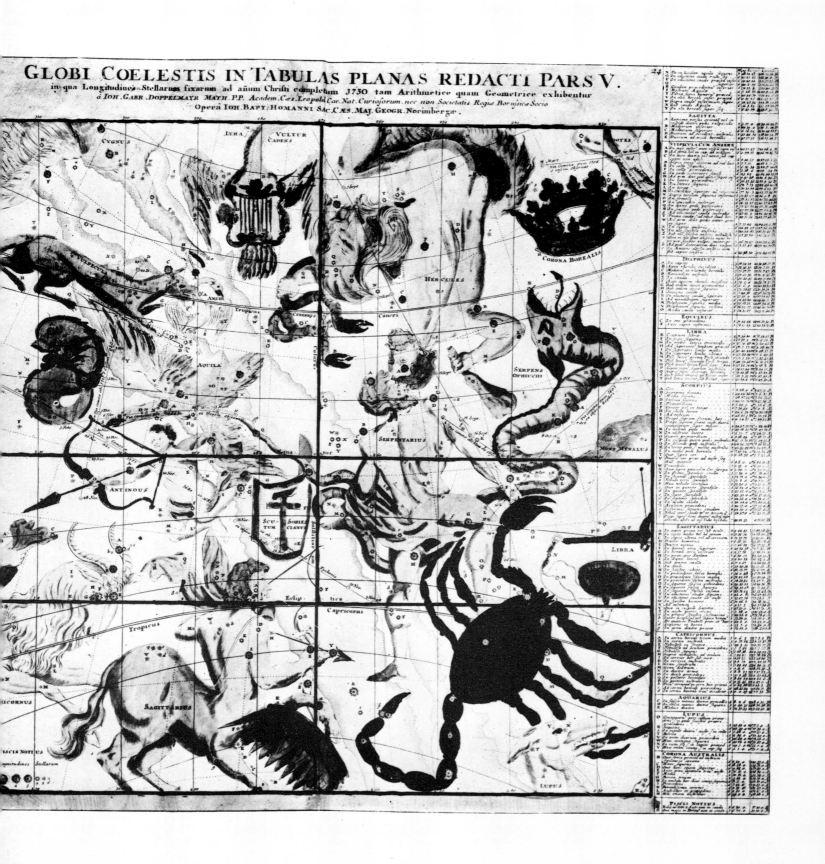

# GLOBI COELESTIS IN TABULAS PLANAS REDACTI PARS V.

in qua Longitudines Stellarum fixarum ad annum Christi completum 1730 tam Arithmetice quam Geometrice exhibentur

à IOH. GABR. DOPPELMAYR MATH. P.P. Academ. Cæs. Leopold Car. Nat. Curiosorum, nec non Societatis Regiæ Borußicæ Socio

Operâ IOH. BAPT. HOMANNI SAC. CÆS. MAJ. GEOGR. Norimbergæ.

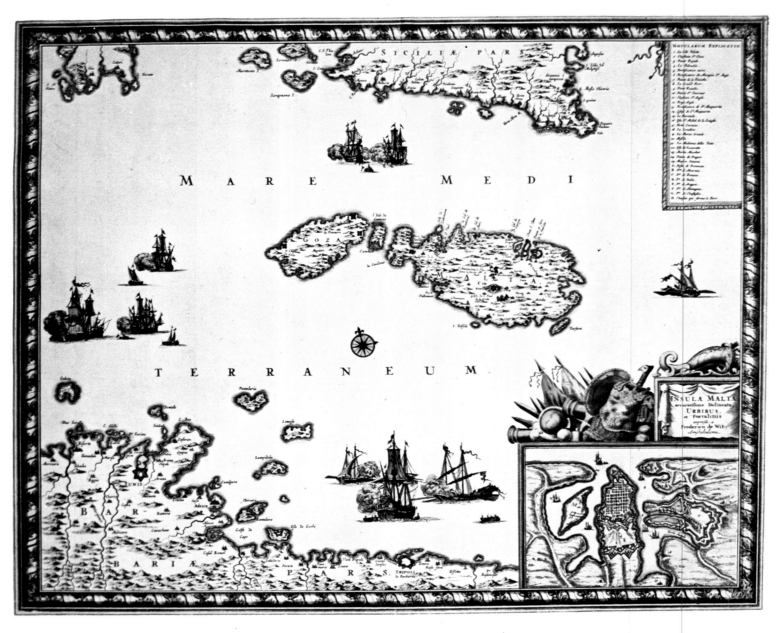

*'Insula Malta.'* *Antique map by F. de Wit*
*showing Malta, the island of Gozo, part of*
*Sicily and N. Africa, with inset plan of*
*Valletta Harbour and numbered key to points of*
*interest. Decorated with cartouche, battle, and*
*local ships. Size of original 17½ × 21⅛ ins.*
*Published in Amsterdam* c 1675. (P)

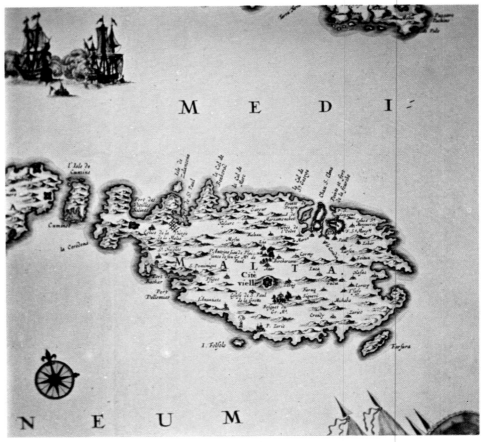

*Enlarged view of 'Insula Malta'.* (P)

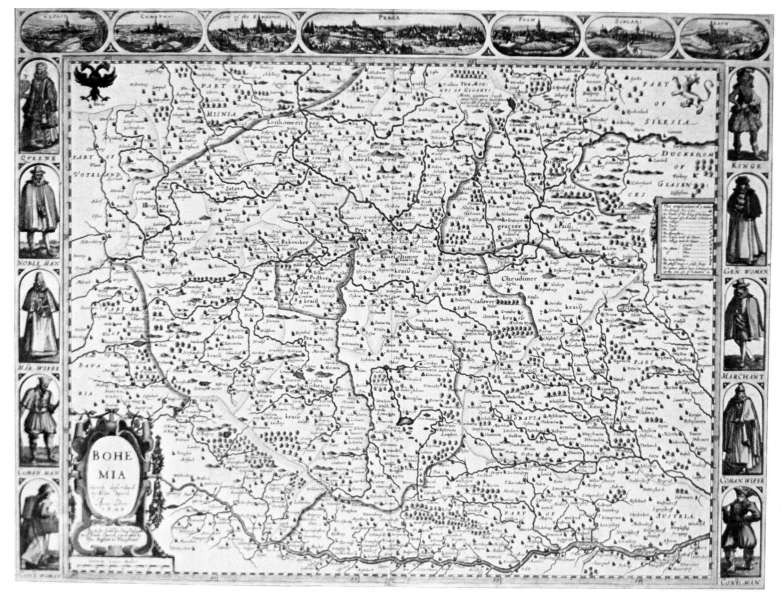

'Bohemia'. This map, by John Speed, is decorated with views of 'Czalsa, Comethar, Praga, Polm, Schlani, Laun', the 'Corte of the Emperor' and with figures of the King and Queen and other lesser nationals such as a 'Marchant' and a 'Coman Man'. Size of original 16½ × 20¾ ins. The date (1626) engraved in the cartouche is the original date of the plate. The lower cartouche scroll encompasses the names of Richard Chiswell and Thomas Bassett, mapsellers who acquired the plates at a later date, probably c 1676. (CT)

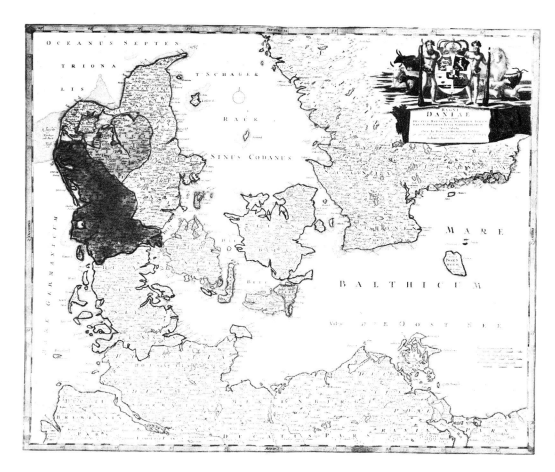

'Regni Daniae.' An antique map of the Kingdom of Denmark by J. B. Homann, decorated with a cartouche of cattle, coat-of-arms and ancient warriors. Size of original 19 × 22⅝ ins. Published c 1720. (N)

The *Abruzzi*. Map by
Joan Blaeu, decorated with large cartouche
and small ships. Size of original 15 × 19⅝ ins.
Published in 1648. (N)

Opposite: *Northern part of Russia in Europe.
The map, by Matthäus Seutter, shows the
Barents Sea (Mare Moscoviti) in the north
and the White Sea (Mare Album). In the
north-west corner is the Kola Peninsula and,
further south, Lakes Ladoga and Onega.* (CT)

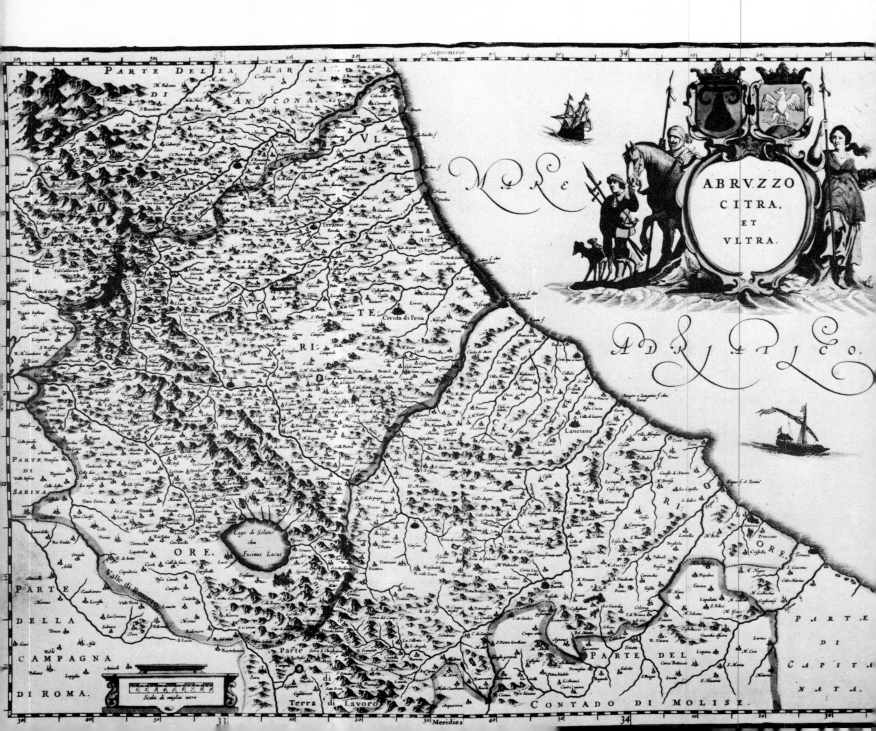

*'Picardia.' Map by Henri du Sauzet. Size of
original 7⅛ ×9⅞ ins. Published in 1734.* (N)

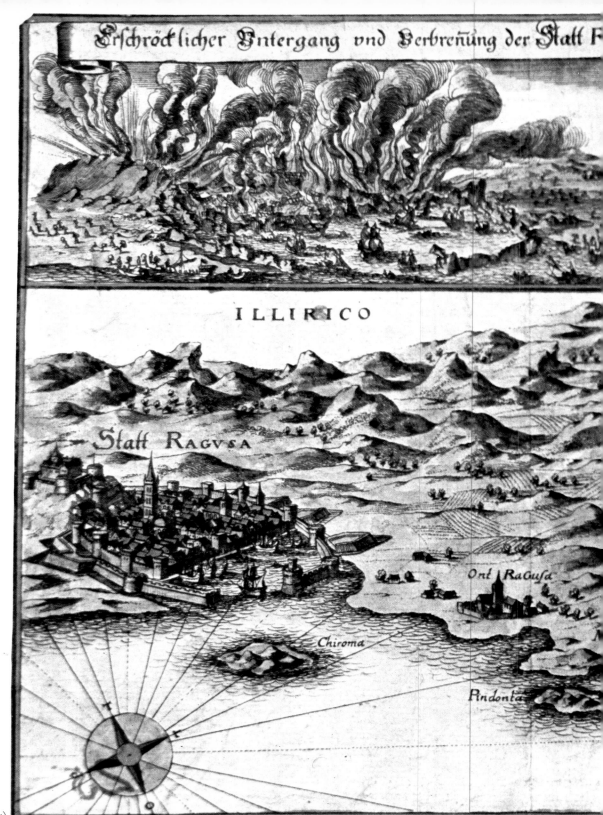

Erschröcklicher Untergang vnd Berbrennung der Statt F...

ILLIRICO

Statt RAGVSA

Chiroma

Ont RaGusa

Pindonta

Part of Illyria. This antique coloured map is of German origin and shows the area around Ragusa (Italian name for Dubrovnik) and the Bay of Kotor. The inset portrays the 'terrible destruction and burning of the city of Ragusa'. Illyria was the name originally given to an ancient region on the east coast of the Adriatic; it became a Roman province from 1st–5th century AD. Size of original 8¼ × 12⅜ ins. (CT)

Spira, now Speyer, in Germany. Map by Sebastian Münster, produced from a woodcut with the place names printed from metal type. Size of original 11½ ×15 ins. Published c 1552.

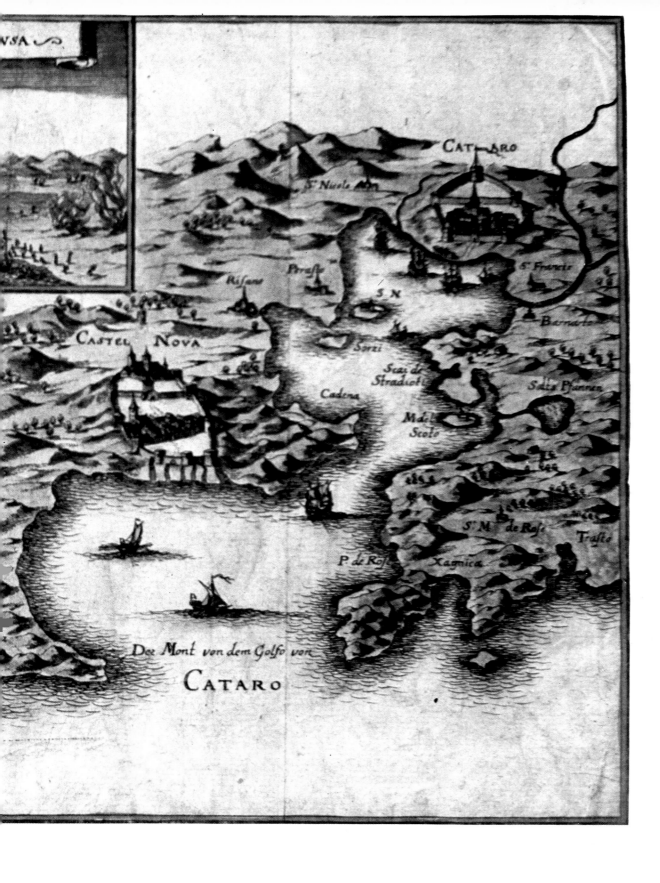

Dee Mont von dem Golfo von
CATARO

*The Kingdom of Naples. Map by J. B. Homann, decorated with an elaborate cartouche. Size of original 22 × 19 ins. Published c 1720.* (N)

*'Ultraiectum Dominium.' A map of Utrecht, Netherlands, by G. Mercator. Size of original 6¾ × 10 ins. Published c 1635.* (N)

*'Denmark.' Map by J. Rapkin with inset views of Copenhagen and Schleswig. Illustrations by H. Warren, engraved by J. B. Allen. Size of original 13 × 9⅞ ins. Published by John Tallis in 1850.* (N)

*Ancient Greece. A coloured map, with an inset
of the northern regions, by J.-B. d'Anville,
decorated with a very delicate cartouche. Size of
original 20¼ × 19½ ins. Published c 1762. (CT)*

*Map of the countries inhabited by the Samoyeds
and the Ostiacs. The land shown is now part of
Northern Russia and includes Novaya Zemlya
(Nouvelle Zemle). Map by Bellin. Size of
original 6¼ × 9½ ins. Published in 1753. (CT)*

Brittany and Normandy. Map by Mercator,
with a boldly patterned sea and fine lettering.
Size of original 7 ⅛ × 9 ¾ ins. Published in 1630. (CT)

Malta and Gozo. Antique map of the two
islands by N. Visscher with inset plan of the
Mediterranean decorated with cartouche and
sailing ships. Size of original 18 ¼ × 22 ⅛ ins. (P)

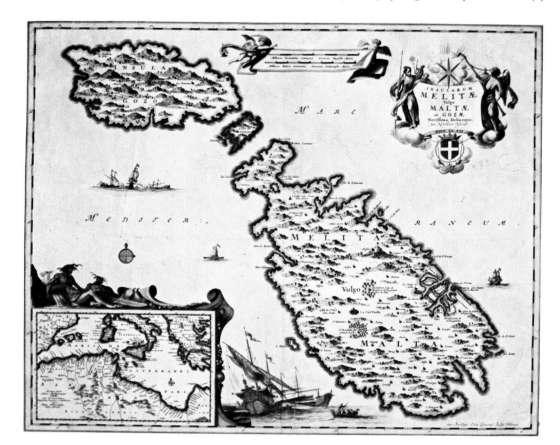

*Italy by Claudius Ptolemaeus (AD c 120–180).*
*A woodcut from the edition by Henricus Petri*
*reprinted in 1545 at Basel.*
*Size of original 12 × 10 ins.* (N)

*Southern Brittany. A chart by Richard Mount*
*showing the coast of France from the Isle of*
*Ushant to below the estuary of the Loire, with*
*inset plans of the Loire as far as Nantes, and*
*Brest Harbour. Size of original 17 ½ × 23 ins.*
*Published in 1729.* (CT)

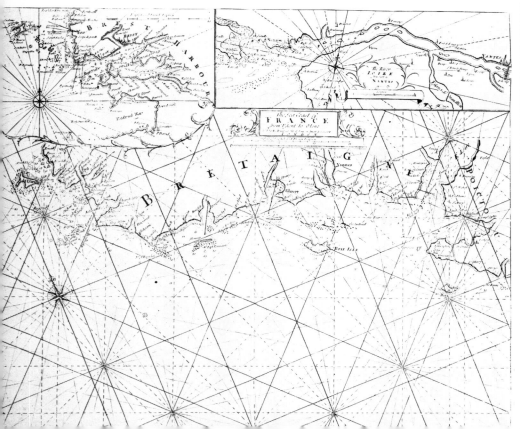

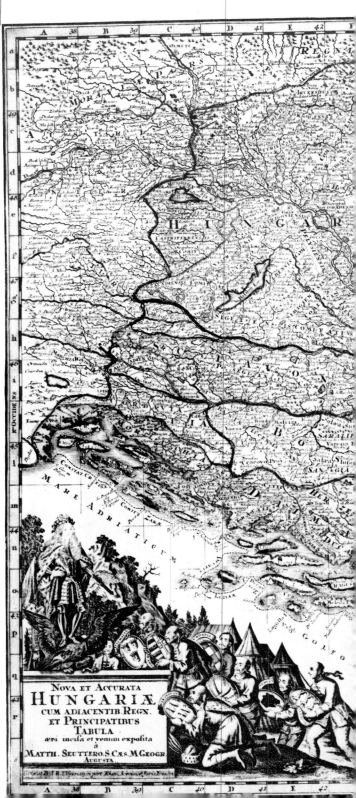

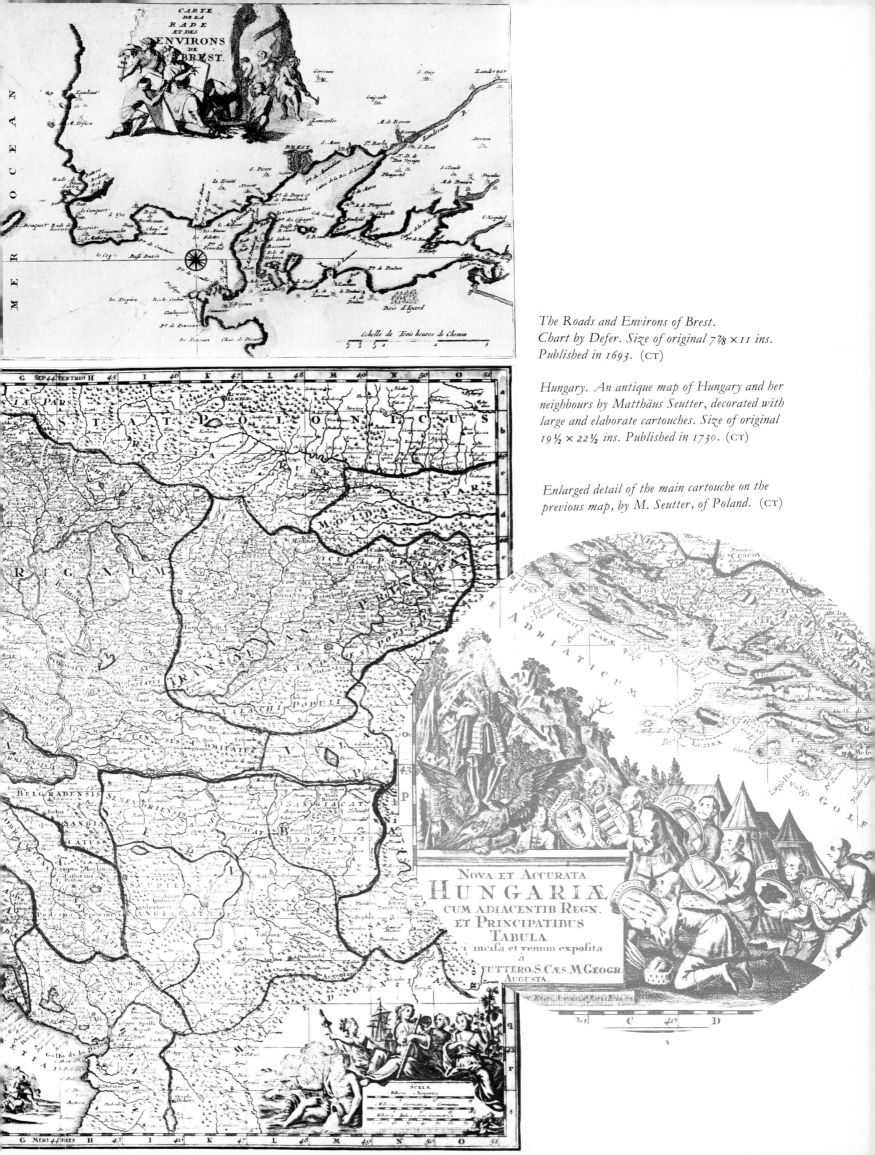

The Roads and Environs of Brest.
Chart by Defer. Size of original 7⅞ × 11 ins.
Published in 1693. (CT)

Hungary. An antique map of Hungary and her
neighbours by Matthäus Seutter, decorated with
large and elaborate cartouches. Size of original
19½ × 22½ ins. Published in 1730. (CT)

Enlarged detail of the main cartouche on the
previous map, by M. Seutter, of Poland. (CT)

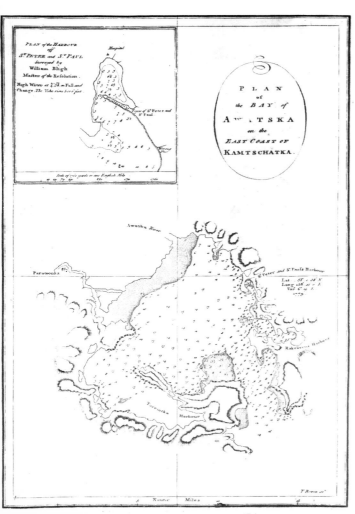

*'Plan of the Bay of Awatska on the East Coast of Kamtschatka.' The map contains an inset plan of the Harbour of St Peter and St Paul surveyed by William Bligh, Master of the Resolution. (This town in the USSR, is now known as Petropavlovsk-Kamchatski.) Published by Alex Hogg in 1784.* (CT)

*St Paul. An old coloured map of the eastern Mediterranean illustrating the travels of St Paul, with nine inset views of incidents from the Acts of the Apostles. Published in Holland c 1680 by N. Visscher.* (CT)

*Enlarged detail of St Paul.* (P)

'Hungari.' An antique map by John Speed, bordered with figures of a Senator, Gentleman, Citizen, Countryman and their women; also with four town views. Published by George Humble in 1627. (N)

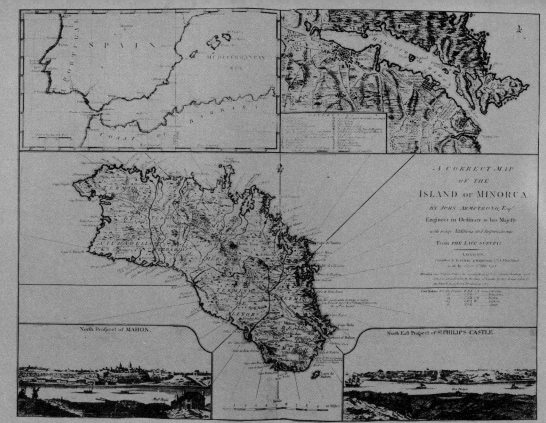

'The Island of Minorca.' This 'correct map' by John Armstrong shows an inset plan of the Western Mediterranean, a more detailed map of Port Mahon and district, a north prospect of Mahon and a north-east prospect of St Philip's Castle. Size of original 17⅜ × 21⅝ ins. Published by Laurie and Whittle in 1799. (N)

'Scandinavia.' This map, by Emanuel Bowen, shows 'the Northern Crowns of Sweden, Denmark, and Norway'. The inset plan on the scroll includes Spitzbergen and Iceland. Size of original 12½ ×9 ins. Published in 1747. (N)

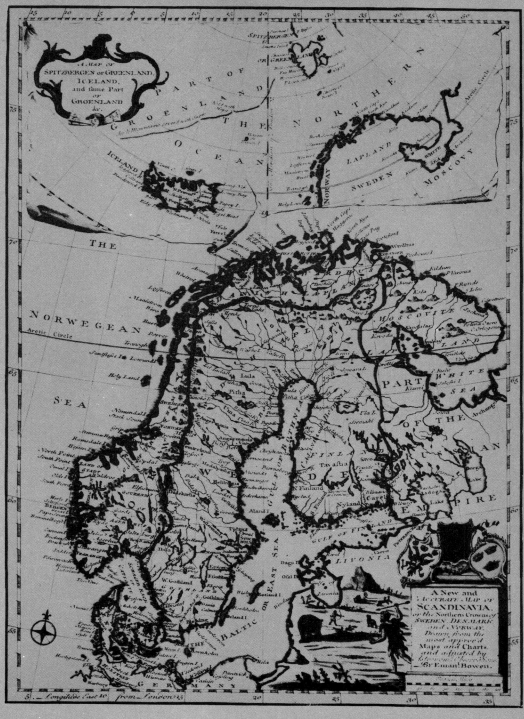

'Poictou.' An antique map of Poitou in France by Abraham Ortelius. Size of original 14¼ × 19¾ ins. Published c 1590. (N)

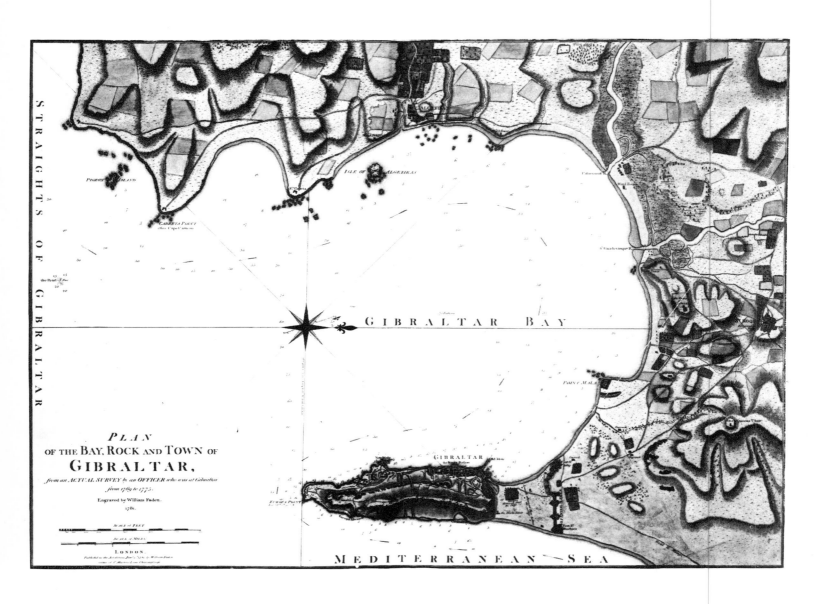

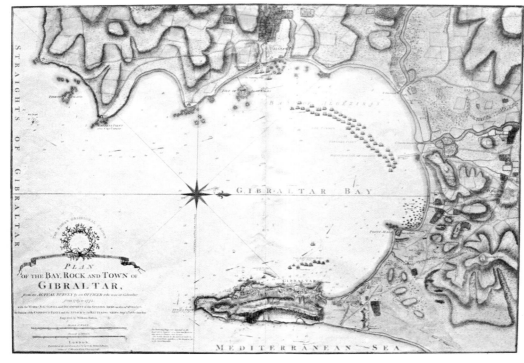

**Above:** *'Plan of the Bay, Rock and Town of Gibraltar.' The map is taken 'from an Actual Survey by an Officer who was at Gibraltar from 1769 to 1775'. Engraved by William Faden. Published in 1781.* (N)

*'Plan of the Bay, Rock and Town of Gibraltar.' This plan by W. Faden shows the encampment of the Spanish Army as on 19 October 1782, and the positions of the enemy's combined fleet and of the battering ships on 13 September in the same year. Size of original 20 × 28½ ins. Published in 1783 by W. Faden.* (CT)

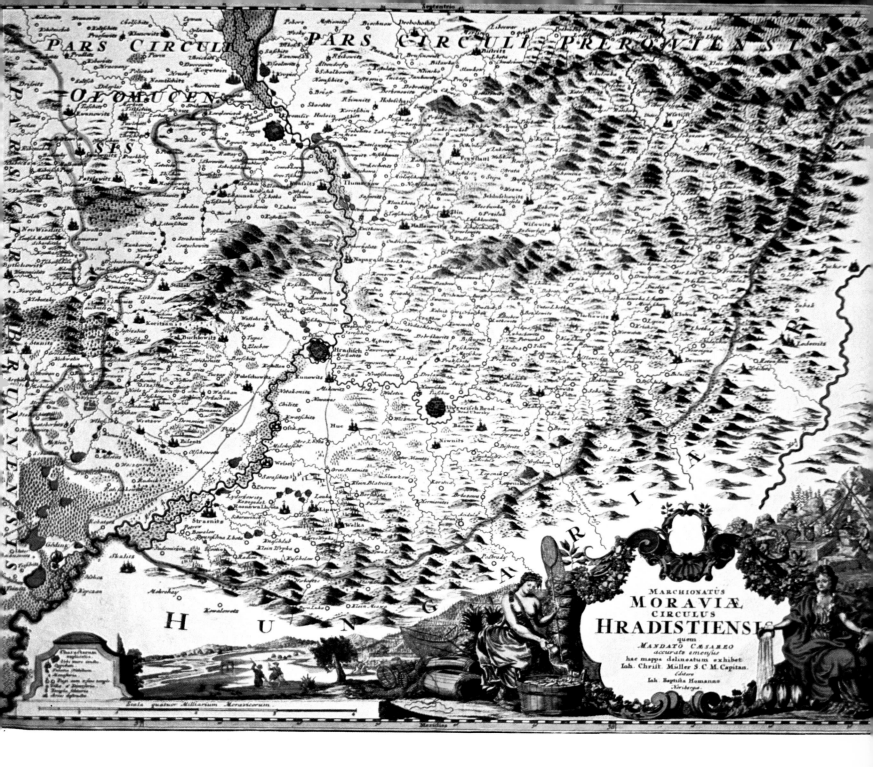

Moravia. Map by J. B. Homann,
decorated with a very large and beautiful
cartouche and explanatory legend.
Size of original 19 × 22¾ ins. (P)

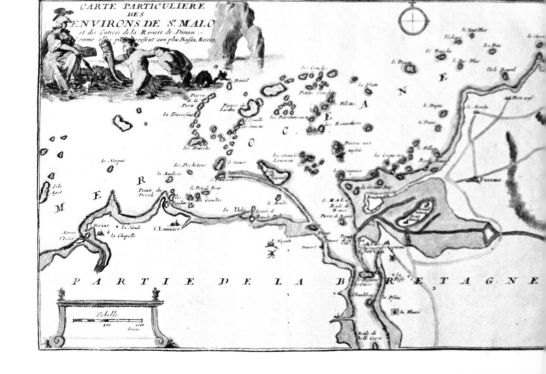

Chart of the Environs of St Malo.
A rather simple but appealing map by Defer
showing the estuary of the Rance. Size of the
original 7½ × 10¾ ins. Published in 1693.

**DVCATO di PARMA et di PIACENZA**

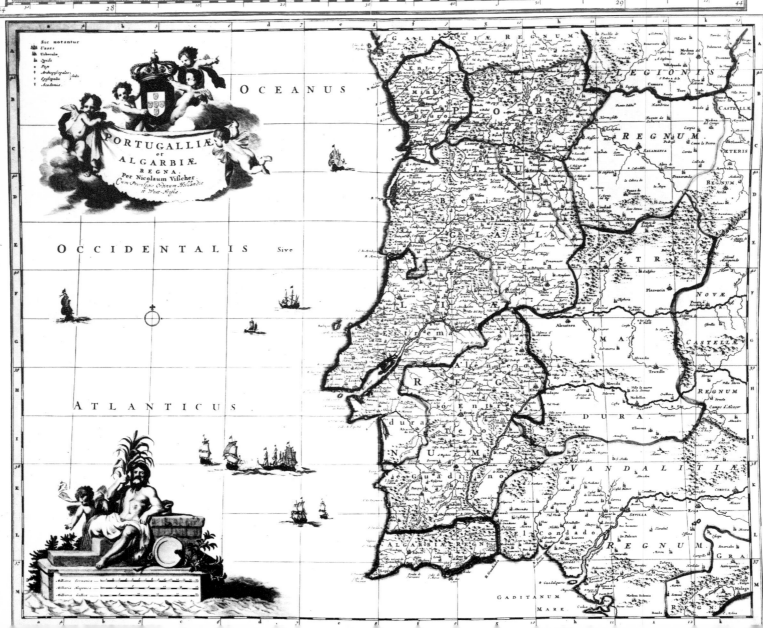

**PORTUGALLIÆ et ALGARBIÆ REGNA.**
Per Nicolaum Visscher

OCEANUS

OCCIDENTALIS Sive

ATLANTICUS

Opposite: *The Duchy of Parma and Piacenza.*
*Map by Joan Blaeu. Size of original*
*15 × 19¾ ins. Published* c *1660.* (CT)

Below, left: '*Portugalliae et Algarbiae Regna.*'
*A beautiful map by N. Visscher of the*
*Kingdoms of Portugal and the Algarve,*
*decorated with a cartouche embellished with*
*cherubs and coat-of-arms. Beautifully drawn*
*ships are shown off the coast. Size of original*
*18 × 22 ins. Published* c *1690.* (N)

'*A New Map of France divided into one*
*hundred and two departments.*' *Size of original*
*21 ½ × 21⅝ ins. Published by Laurie and*
*Whittle in 1802.* (CT)

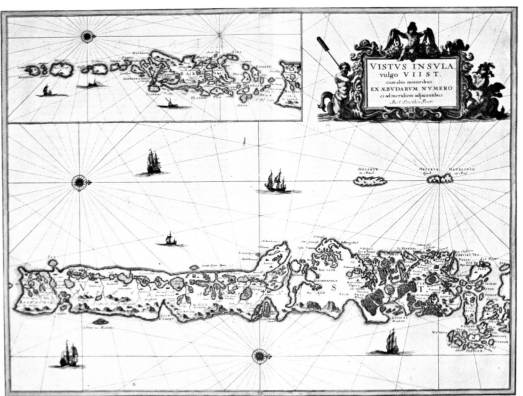

Europe. A 'New Plaine and Exact Map of Europe' by N. Visscher, English edition by J. Blaeu. The borders are decorated with views of London, Prague, Rome, Antwerp, Amsterdam, Paris, Seville, Danzig, Stockholm, and Hamburg, and with figures of men and women representing various nations, also heads of the Kings of Spain, France, Sweden and Denmark. Size of original 16¼ × 20¾ ins. Published by Robert Walton. (CT)

The Islands of Uist in the Outer Hebrides, with inset map of Barra. Size of original 17¾ × 22¾ ins. Engraved by Timothy Pont. Published by Blaeu in 1650. (CT)

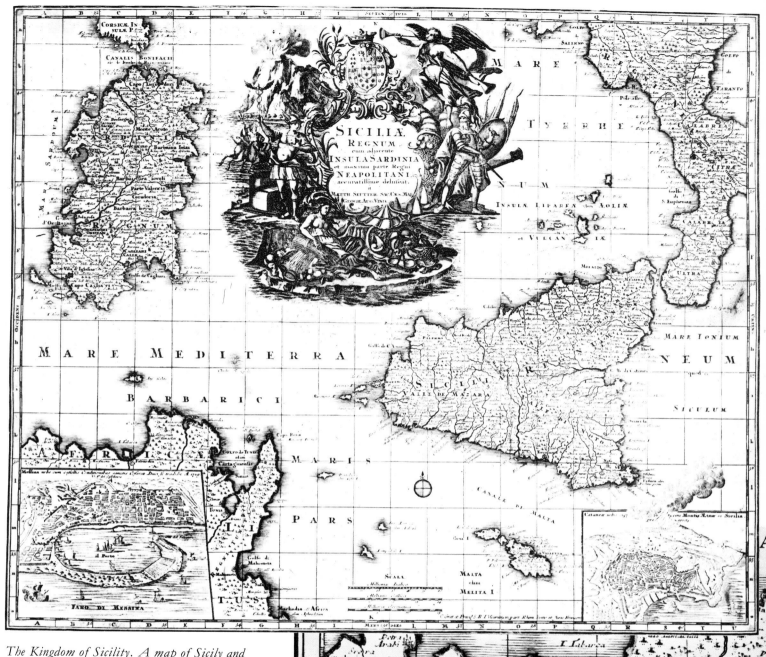

The Kingdom of Sicily. A map of Sicily and
Sardinia by Matthäus Seutter, decorated with a
large and elaborate cartouche, also inset views of
Catania, with Mt Etna in background, and
Messina. Size of original 19¼ × 22¾ ins.
Published in 1730. (CT)

Enlarged inset detail of Messina from the
previous map of Sicily by M. Seutter. (CT)

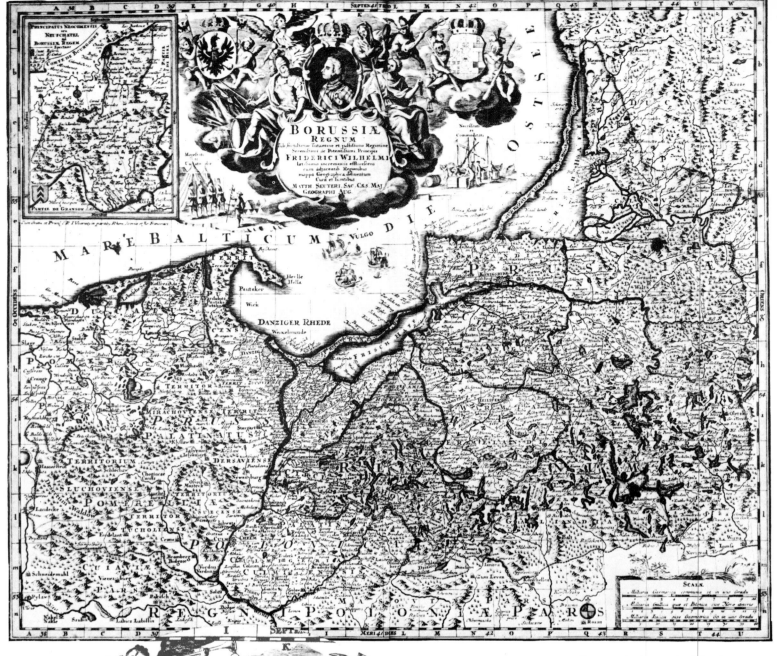

'Borussiae Regnum.' *A map by Matthäus Seutter of the country now known as Poland, decorated with an elaborate cartouche. Size of original 19¼ × 22⅝ ins. Published in 1730.* (CT)

*Enlarged detail of the main cartouche on the previous map of Hungary by M. Seutter.* (CT)

Opposite, top: 'Navarra Regnum.' *An antique map of Navarre, Spain, by Joan Blaeu decorated with various coats-of-arms and an elaborate cartouche. Size of original 16½ × 19¾ ins. Published in 1662.*

Opposite: *The Margraviate of Brandenburg and the Duchies of Pomerania and Mecklenburg. An antique map by Matthäus Seutter showing the northern coasts of Poland and Germany. Size of original 19¼ × 22½ ins. Published in 1730.* (CT)

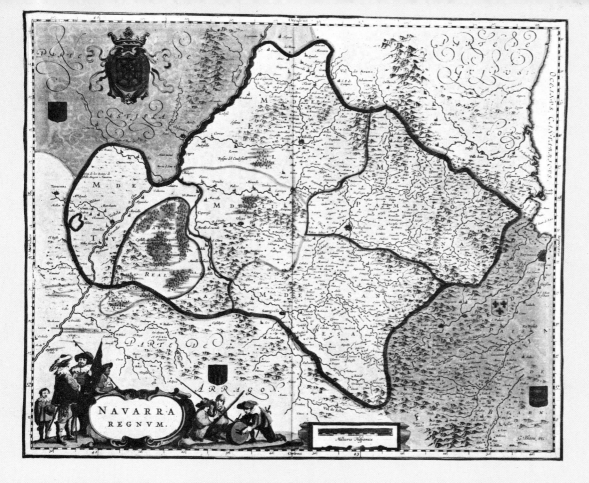

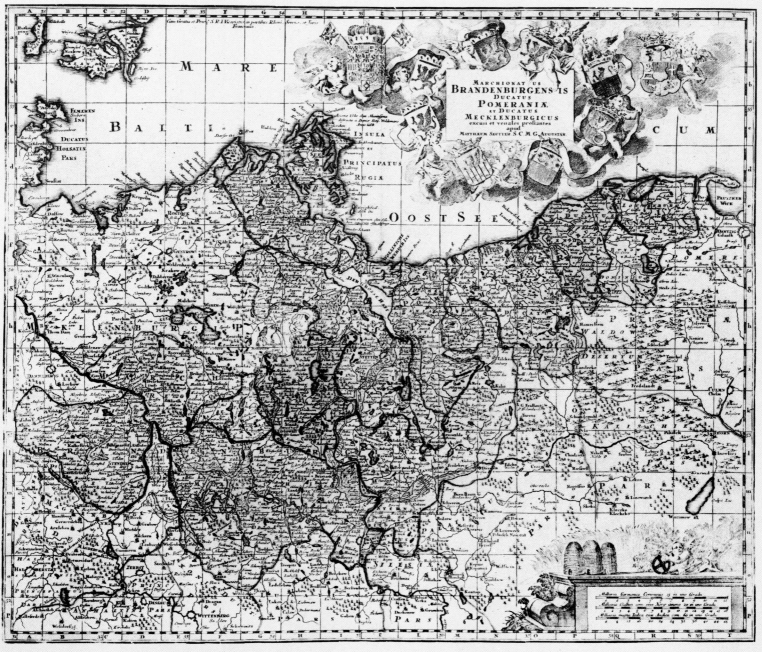

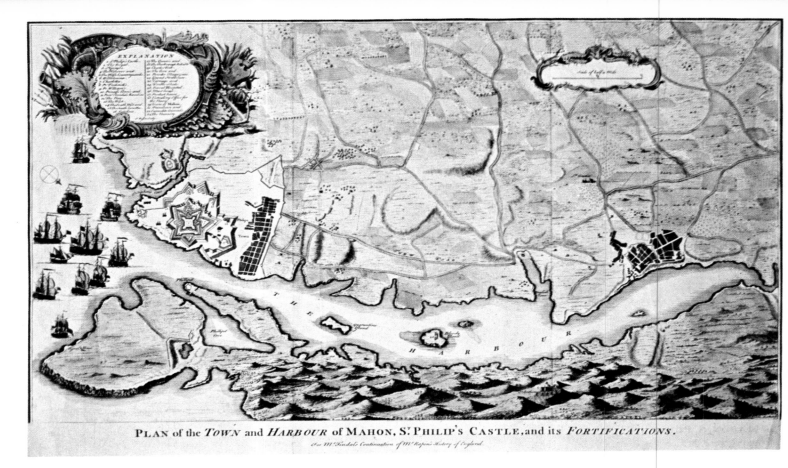

PLAN of the *TOWN* and *HARBOUR* of MAHON, S.* PHILIP'S CASTLE, and its *FORTIFICATIONS*.

*One M.* Tindals Continuation of M.* Rapins History of England.

'Plan of the Town and Harbour of Mahon, St Philip's Castle, and its Fortifications.' This attractive map of Minorca's principal town was prepared and published during the period from 1713–1802 when Britain controlled the strategically valuable Balearics – hence the strong naval presence. The fortifications are clearly defined. The map is decorated with an elaborate cartouche of foliage, and ships in the famous natural harbour. Size of original 13½ × 24½ ins. Engraved by J. Basire. Published in 1739 for 'Mr Tindal's Continuation of Mr Rapkin's History of England'. (CT)

'Italia'. Map by Matthäus Seutter. Tinted with original colour, the provinces have been treated by a wash, but the beautiful cartouche has been left uncoloured. Size of original 19⅜ × 22¾ ins. Published in 1730. (CT)

Above: Map of the Journeys of Aeneas. This coloured map of the Mediterranean claims to note every place-name mentioned in the works of Virgil 'for a better understanding of that author'. Size of original 14⅝ × 19¾ ins. Published in Paris by P. Mariette. (P)

Below: Finistère. An extremely decorative map of the French department with inset panels providing Statistics, Curiosities, Celebrities, Commercial details and a key to the symbols used. This is one of a series by V. Levasseur. Size of original 11⅛ × 16¾ ins. Published in Paris c 1845. (P)

DÉP.t DU FINISTÈRE.

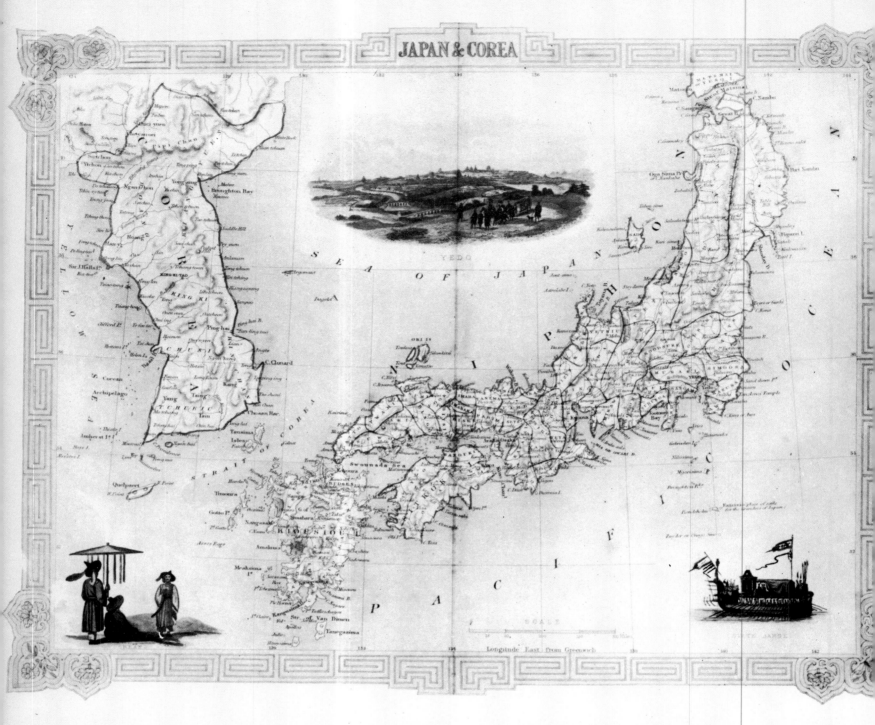

'Japan and Corea.' Map by J. Rapkin with
views of 'Yedo' (Tokyo), a state barge and a
group of 'native Coreans'. Illustrations by
H. Warren, engraved by J. Kernot.
Size of original 10 × 12 ins. Published by
J. Tallis in 1850. (N)


Opposite, top: The Ukraine. Map by
Moses Pitt. Size of original 15 × 19½ ins.
Published c 1670. (N)


Opposite: The Empire of the Moguls. This map
shows the empire extending over north and central
India and much of Afghanistan. It is decorated
with a small cartouche, ships and elephants.
Size of original 16⅜ × 20½ ins. Published by
Joan and Cornelius Blaeu in c 1660. (N)

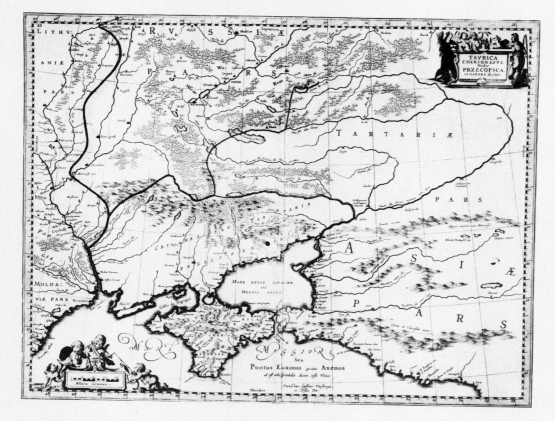

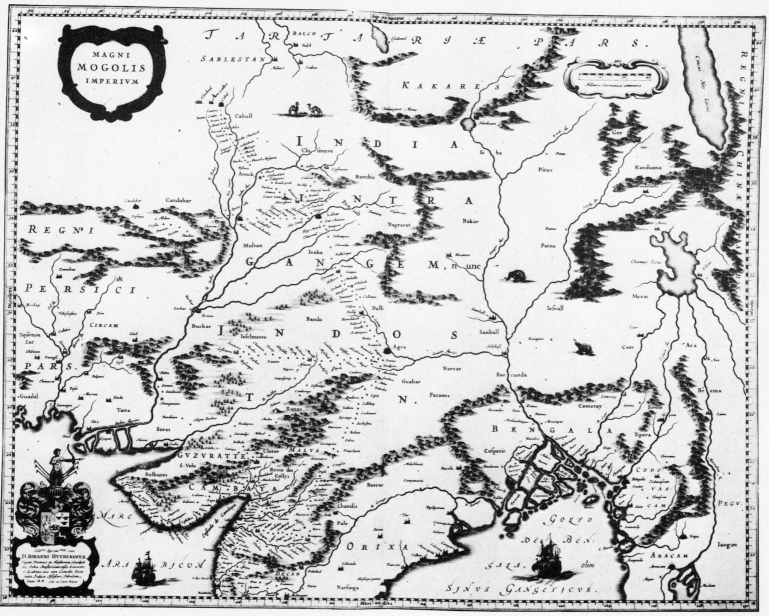

*Tartary. Map by M. Merian. Size of original 10½ × 13¾ ins. Published in 1646. (N)*

*Asia. A companion to Europe. A 'New Plaine and Exact Map of Europe', also by N. Visscher, English-language version by J. Blaeu. The borders are decorated with views of Aden, Jerusalem, Goa, Macao, etc., and with figures in native costume; also featured are the heads of the Kings of Tartary, China, Ceylon, Persia, Turkey and the Moluccas. Size of original 16⅜ × 20¾ ins. Published by Robert Walton. (CT)*

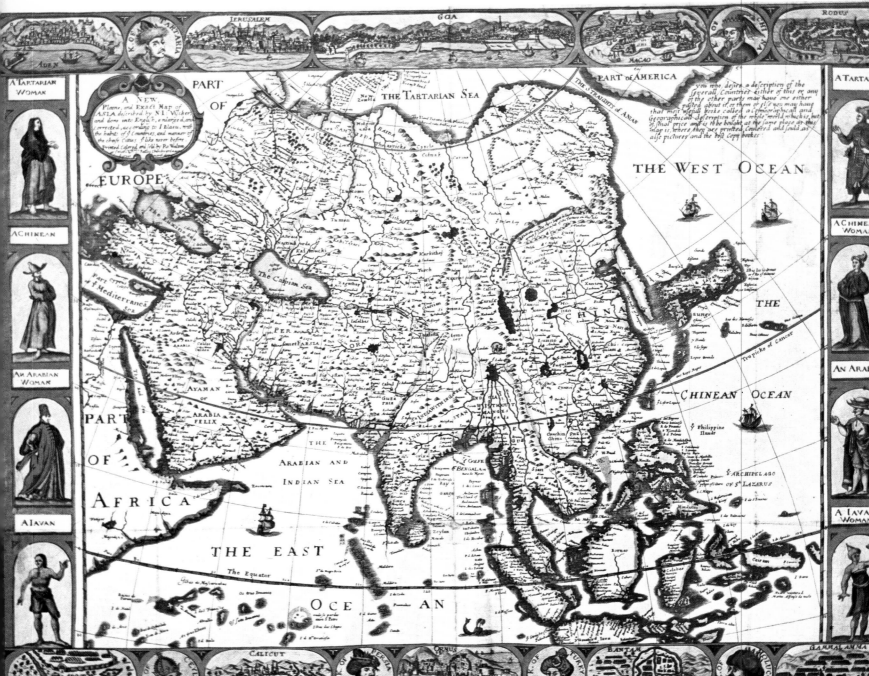

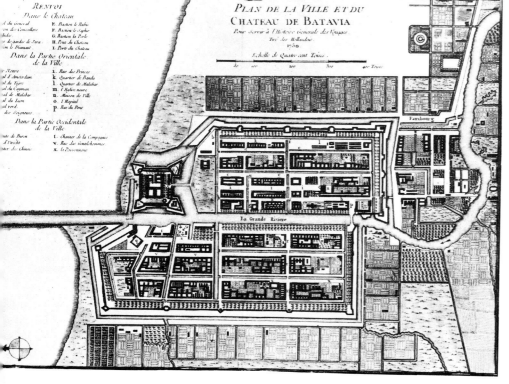

'The Empire of Japan Divided into Seven
Principal Parts and Subdivided into Sixty
Kingdoms, with the Kingdom of Corea
(Korea).' A coloured map, size of original
18¾ × 25 ins. Published by Laurie and
Whittle about 1800. (CT)

Batavia (Jakarta). Plan of the town and
castle by J. Bellin. Size of original
8½ × 11¾ ins. Published c 1750.

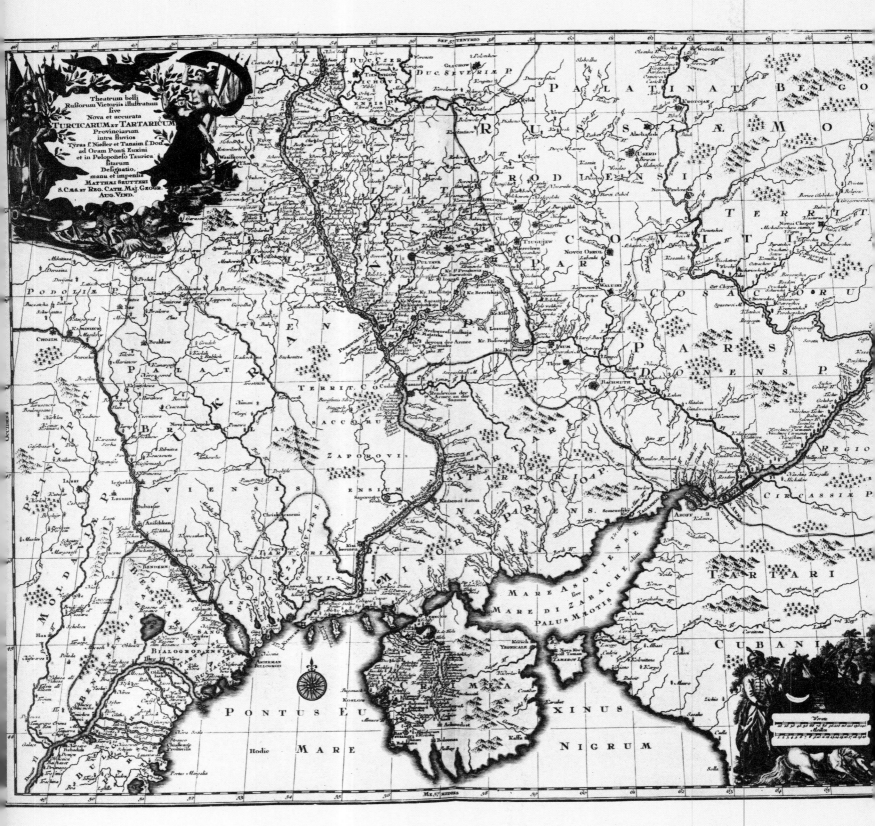

'Turcicarum et Tartaricum.'
An antique map by Matthäus Seutter of the
Ukraine and the Crimea, decorated with two
cartouches. Size of original 19¼ × 22½ ins.
Published c 1740. (N)

'Japonia.' *An antique map by Mercator of Japan showing a part of China and Korea. Produced with little ships, sea monsters and fine scroll decoration. Size of original 13½ × 17⅝ ins. Published c 1628.* (CT)

Left: *Detail from Mercator's map of Japan.* (CT)

65

EU A PARIS Chez Mariette ROPAE MARE TARTARICUM AMERICÆ PARS ASIA RECENS nimia cura delineata

PARS OCEANUS OCCIDENTALIS

GRÆCIA NOVA ZEMBLA

OCE

ANUS

CHINENSIS

AFRI Philippinæ Insulæ

ARABIA DESERTA

ARABIA FELIX ARCHIPELAGUS S. LAZARI

CÆ PARS MARE ARABICUM et INDICUM GOLFO DI BENGALA

OCEANUS

ORIEN Ceylan

TALIS

A CORRECT MAP of the OTTOMAN EMPIRE, Including all the Countries, Possess'd by, or Tributary to the TURKS, IN EUROPE, ASIA & AFRICA, with part of the Adjacent Territories, according to the latest Observations by Thos Bowen

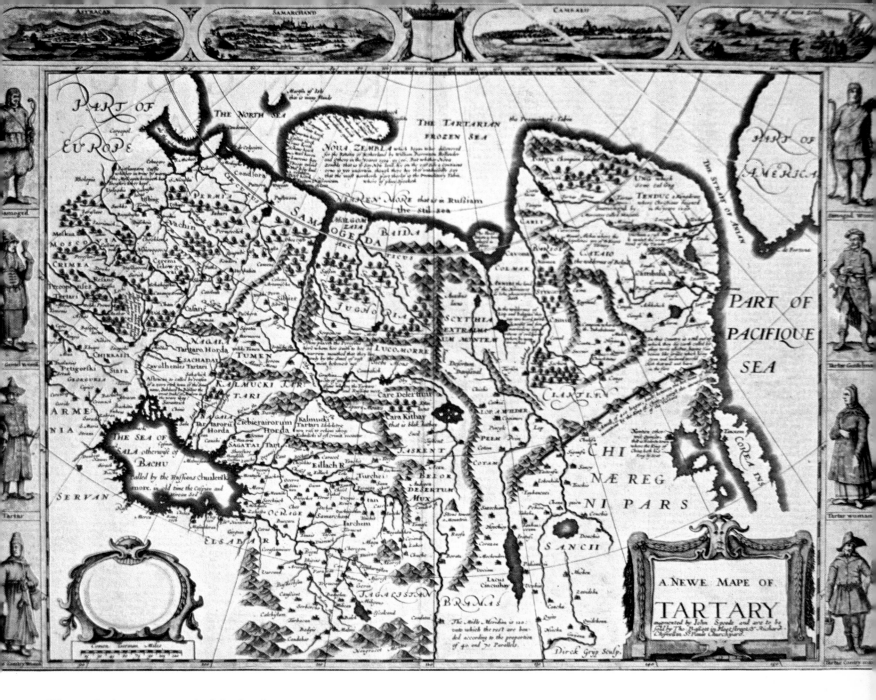

'Tartary.' *An antique map by John Speed*
*of Russia in Asia, with border decorations*
*of figures and inset views of 'Astracan*
*Samarchand, Cambalu and a (Samoyed) house*
*of Nova Zemla'. Size of original 15½ × 20 ins.*
*Published by Bassett and Chiswell.* (P)

Opposite, top: '*Asia Recens.' Map by*
*Pierre Mariette. Size of original 13¾ × 17¾ ins.*
*Published* c *1650.* (N)

'*A Correct Map of the Ottoman Empire*
*Including all the Countries, Possess'd by,*
*or Tributary to the Turks, in Europe,*
*Asia & Africa.' Map by Thomas Bowen.*
*Size of original 12¼ × 16½ ins.*
*Published in 1788.* (CT)

67

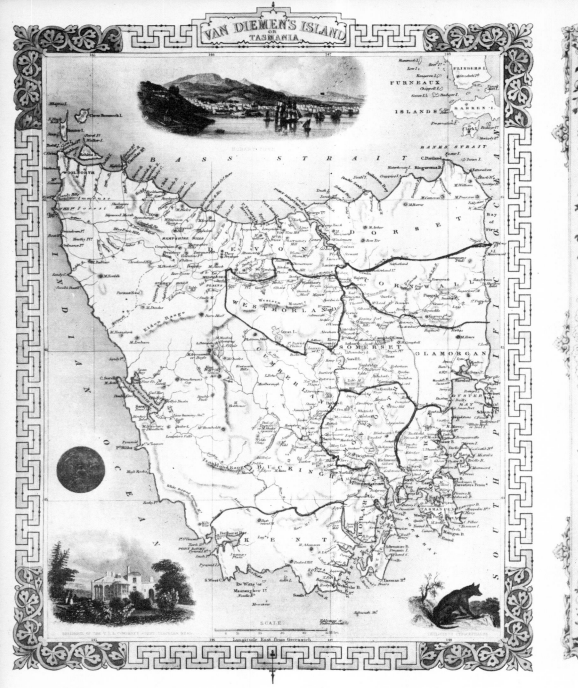

'*Van Diemen's Island or Tasmania.*' The map
includes inset views of Hobart Town, the
residence of the Van Diemen's Land Company's
agent, and a Thylacine or Tasmanian Wolf.
Size of original  13¾ × 10¼ ins. Map drawn
and engraved by J. Rapkin. Illustrations by
H. Warren and engraved by J. Rogers.
Published by John Tallis c 1850. (CT)

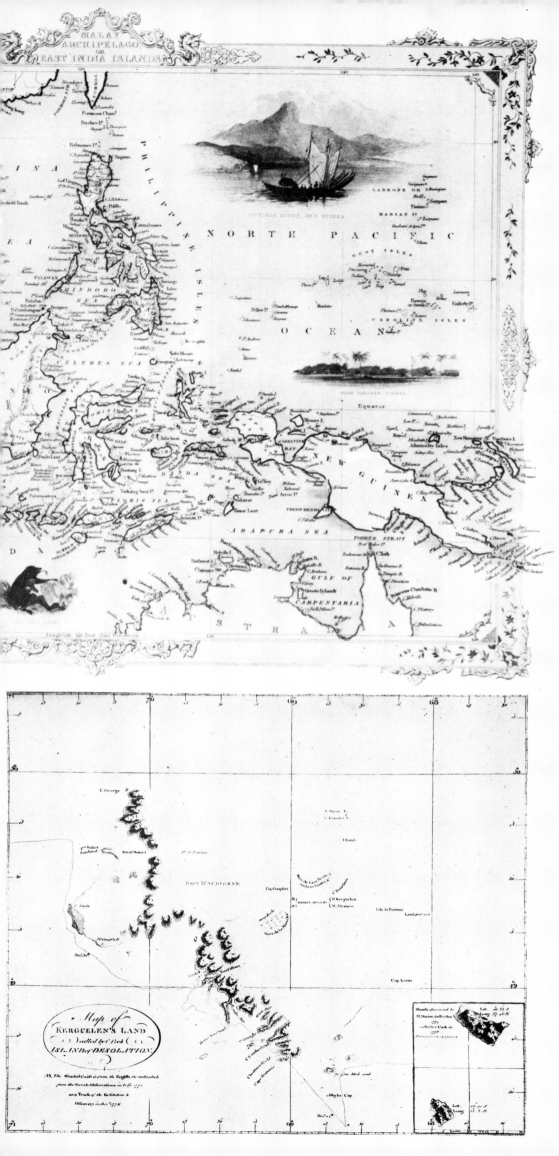

'Malay Archipelago or East India Islands.'
This map is decorated with a view of Victoria
Mount, New Guinea, another near Sarawak,
and with figures representing natives of New
Guinea, and 'the Bee Bear', presumably a
popular name for the honey-eating Malayan or
Sun Bear. The illustrations, by H. Warren,
are engraved by T. Smith. Map drawn and
engraved by J. Rapkin. Size of original
10½ × 13½ ins. Published in 1850. (CT)

'Map of Kerguelen's Land.' A map of the main
island in this archipelago in the Indian Ocean,
called by Captain Cook 'Island of Desolation'.
The inset features the Prince Edward Isles.
This map shows the route taken in 1776 by the
Resolution and Discovery. Size of original
9 × 10¾ ins. Published by A. Hogg in 1784. (CT)

# NEW ZEALAND

'New Zealand.' Map drawn and engraved by
J. Rapkin. Illustrations by H. Warren,
engraved by J. B. Allan. Size of original
12½ × 9⅝ ins. Published by J. Tallis in 1850. (CT)


'A Chart of the Pacific Ocean.' A chart
surveying recent discoveries in the region.
Size of original 9 × 13 ins. Published in 1825. (CT)

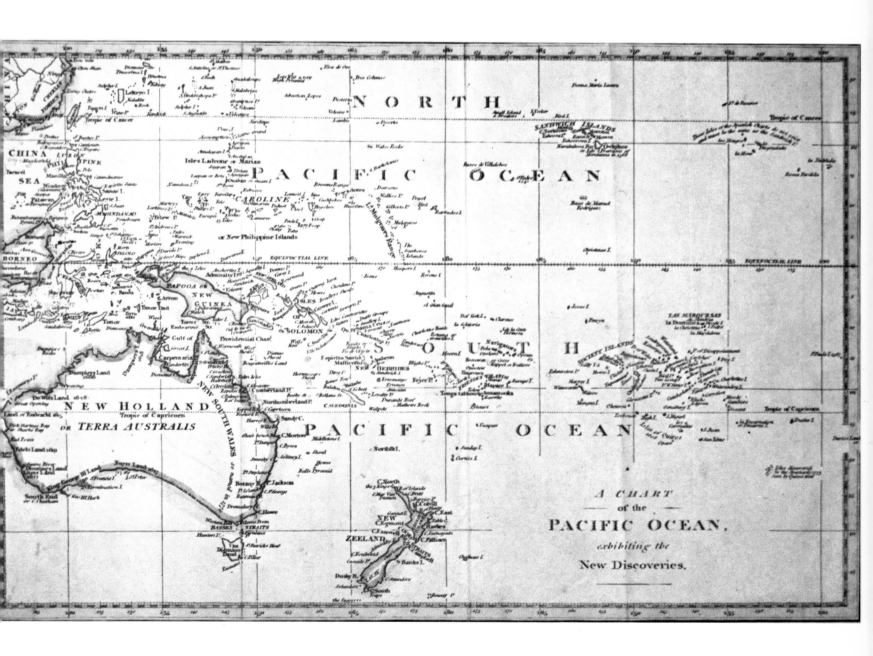

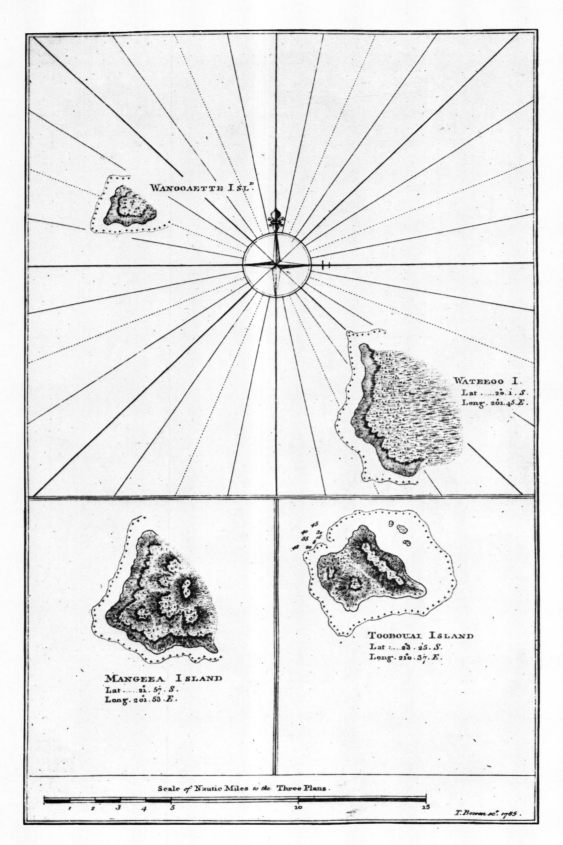

Islands of the Pacific. Three maps on a single
sheet showing Wanooaette Island and Wateeoo
Island, Mangeea Island, and Toobouai Island
(Tubuai). Size of original 12½ × 8 ins.
Engraved by T. Bowen. Published by
Alex Hogg c 1785. (CT)

'Polynesia, or Islands in the Pacific Ocean.'
The map features inset views of the Sandwich
Islands, Tahiti (Otaheite), the Harbour of
Dory, New Guinea, and Resolution Bay in the
Marquesas. Map drawn and engraved by
J. Rapkin. Illustrations by H. Winkles
engraved by T. Weightson. Size of original
10 × 13¼ ins. Published by J. Tallis in 1850. (CT)

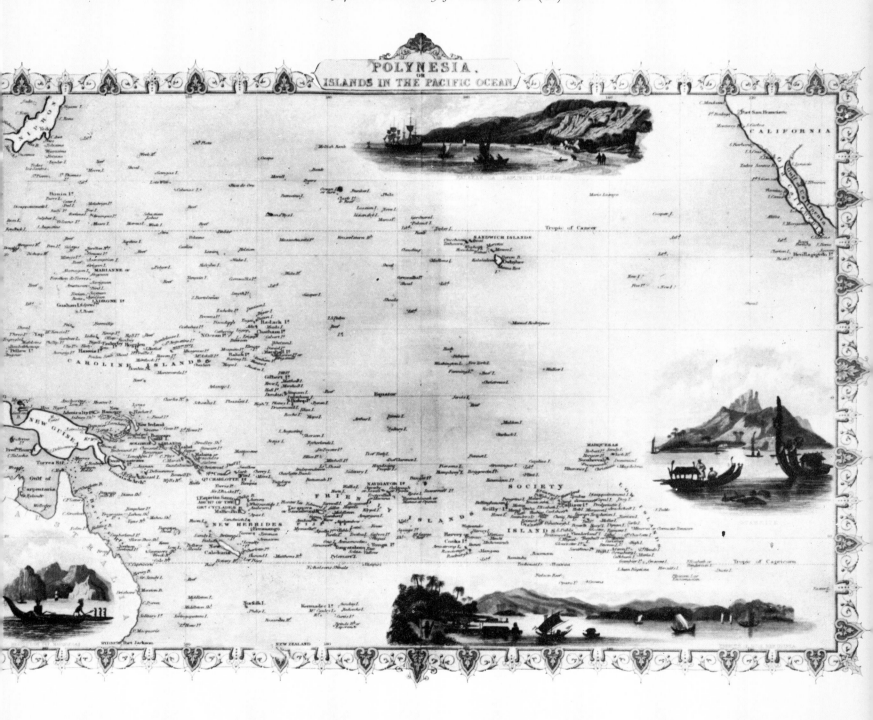

Right: 'Mississippi Territory.' An early
nineteenth-century map by Arrowsmith.
Size of original 7¾ × 9¾ ins. (CT)

Opposite: Carolina. An antique map of
Carolina by A. H. Jaillot. Size of original
19 × 23½ ins. Published in Amsterdam in 1696
by Pieter Mortier. (N)

Below, right: 'Part of South Australia.'
This map was drawn and engraved by
J. Rapkin with illustrations by H. Warren,
engraved by J. Rogers. Size of original
12½ × 9⅝ ins. Published by J. Tallis in 1850. (CT)

'New South Wales.' Map drawn and engraved
by J. Rapkin. Illustrations by H. Warren,
engraved by J. Rogers. Size of original
12⅞ × 9⅞ ins. Published by J. Tallis in 1850
(CT)

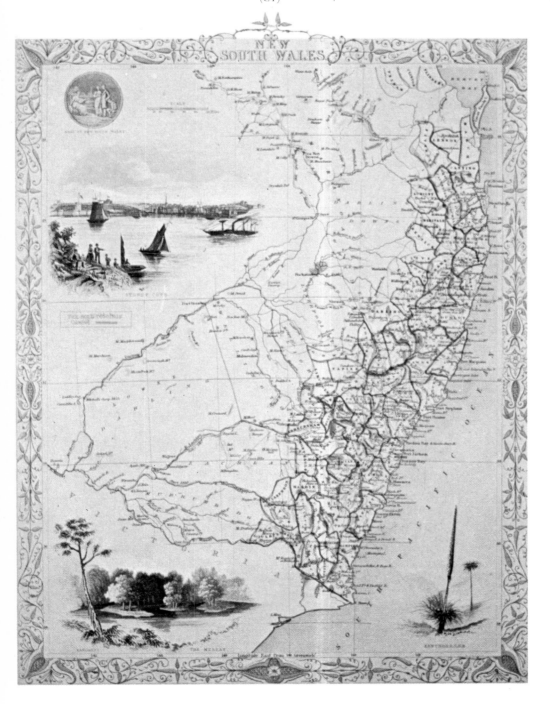

*'America.' Size of original $23\frac{1}{2} \times 18\frac{3}{4}$ ins. Map drawn and
published by J. Arrowsmith c 1835. (N)*

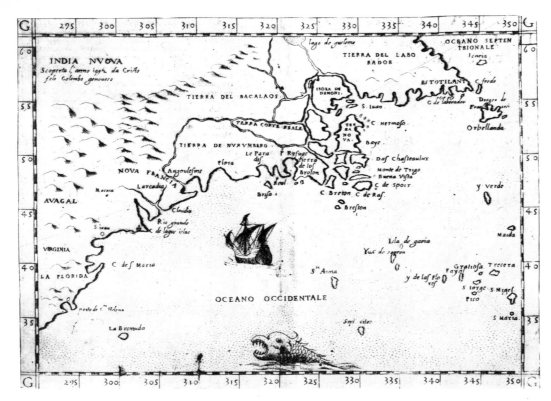

'Tierra Neuva.' New England from the 1599 edition of maps attributed (with dispute) to Ptolemy, published by the heirs of Melchoir Sessa. Size of original 7 × 9½ ins. (This map is presumed to have been copied from the original in Ptolemy's Geographia, a Greek manual on maps written about AD 60.) (N)

'United States.' A small map 7⅜ × 9¾ ins. Engraved by J. C. Russell c 1820. (CT)

'Colton's City of Baltimore.' Size of original
13 × 16 ins. Published in New York by
Johnson and Browning 1855. (CT)

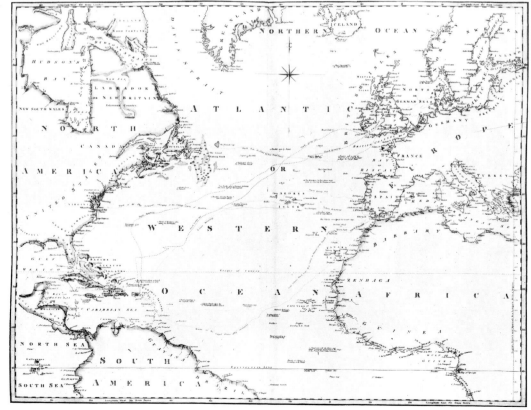

'Chart of North Atlantic Ocean, with tracks
of the Shipping to West Indies, North
America &c.' Size of original 19½ × 25 ins.
Published by Thomsons in 1815. (CT)

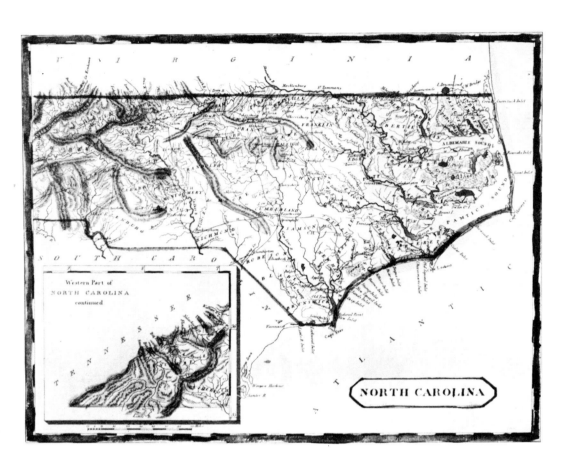

NORTH CAROLINA

Western Part of
NORTH CAROLINA
continued

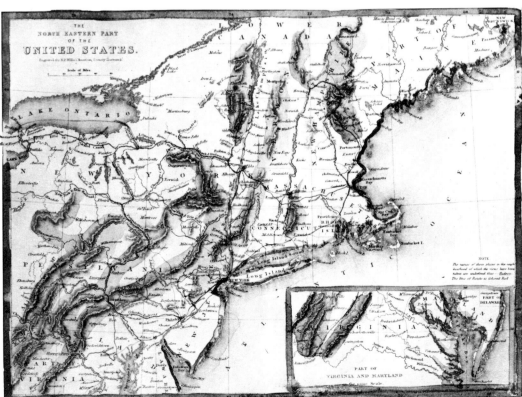

THE
NORTH EASTERN PART
OF THE
UNITED STATES.

PART OF
VIRGINIA AND MARYLAND

Part of the STATE of NEW YORK.

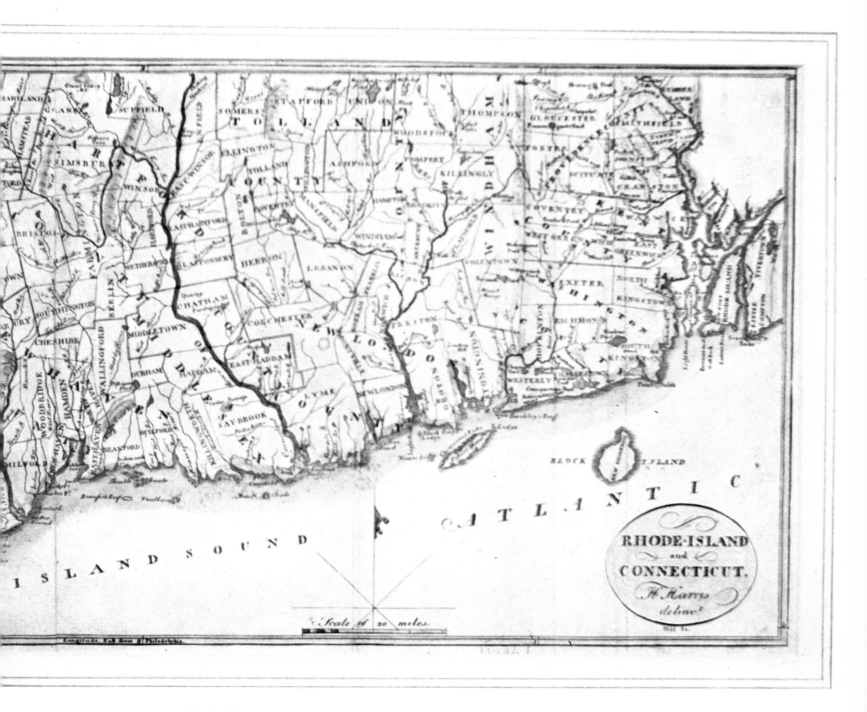

'Rhode Island and Connecticut.' Map by
H. Harris. Size of original 7½ × 13 ins.
Engraved by Hill. Published by Thomas
and Andrews, Boston. (P)

Opposite, top: 'North Carolina.' This map
has an inset view of the western part of the state.
Size of original 7¾ × 9¾ ins. Published in
1812 by Arrowsmith. (CT)

Opposite: 'The North Eastern Part of the
United States.' Size of original 7¼ × 9½ ins.
Engraved for N. P. Willis's American
Scenery Illustrated. Published in London
by G. Virtue c 1840. (CT)

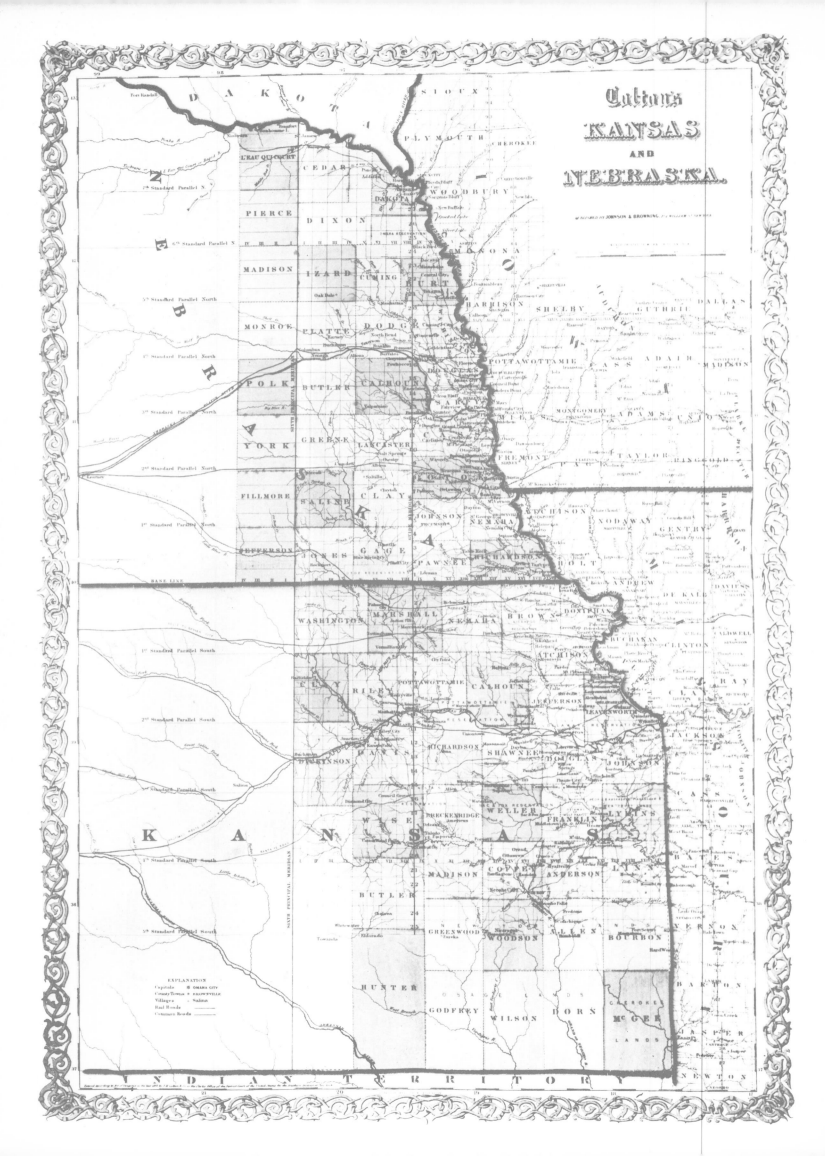

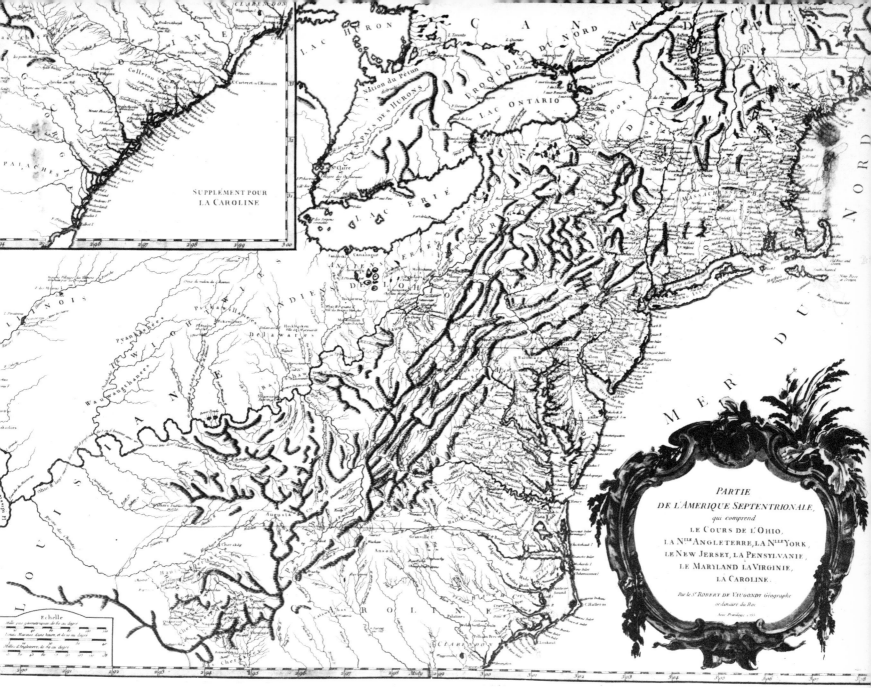

SUPPLÉMENT POUR
LA CAROLINE

PARTIE
DE L'AMERIQUE SEPTENTRIONALE,
qui comprend
LE COURS DE L'OHIO,
LA N<sup>lle</sup> ANGLETERRE, LA N<sup>lle</sup> YORK,
LE NEW JERSEY, LA PENSYLVANIE,
LE MARYLAND, LA VIRGINIE,
LA CAROLINE.

Par le S<sup>r</sup> ROBERT DE VAUGONDY Géographe
ordinaire du Roi

*Part of North America. A Map by
Robert de Vaugondy showing the eastern
territories between the River Ohio and the
Atlantic: these include New England,
New York, New Jersey, Pennsylvania,
Maryland, Virginia and Carolina. Size of
original 18½ × 24¼ ins. Published in 1757.* (N)

*Right: The south-eastern states of the USA.
An early nineteenth-century map by John Cary
'containing the Carolinas and Georgia, also the
Floridas and part of the Bahama Islands &c.'
Size of original 18 × 20⅜ ins.
Published in 1806.* (N)

*Left: 'Colton's Kansas and Nebraska.'
Size of original 25¼ × 16⅝ ins.
Published in New York by Johnson and
Browning c 1857.* (CT)

NEW MAP
of part of the
UNITED STATES
of
NORTH AMERICA
containing the
CAROLINAS AND GEORGIA.
Also the FLORIDAS and part
of the
BAHAMA ISLANDS &c.

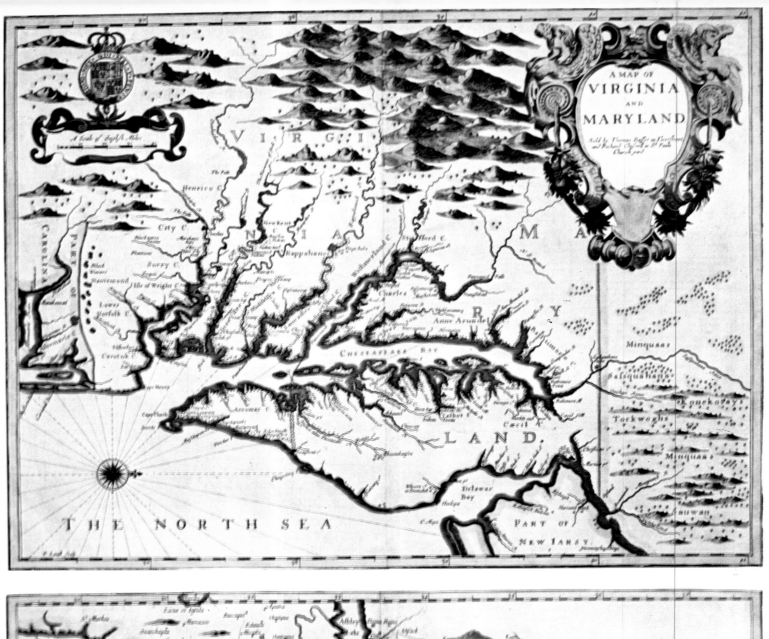

Opposite: 'A Map of Virginia and Maryland.'
This Map, by John Speed, looks westward (inland
from the Atlantic coast, here described as the
'North Sea'. Size of original 14¾ × 19¼ ins.
Engraved by F. Lamb and published in 1676
by Bassett and Chiswell. (N)

'The River Mississippi.' The map shows the
course of the river from the sea past New
Orleans to Bayagoulas. Size of original
7 × 9 ½ ins. Published for the London
Magazine c 1760. (P)

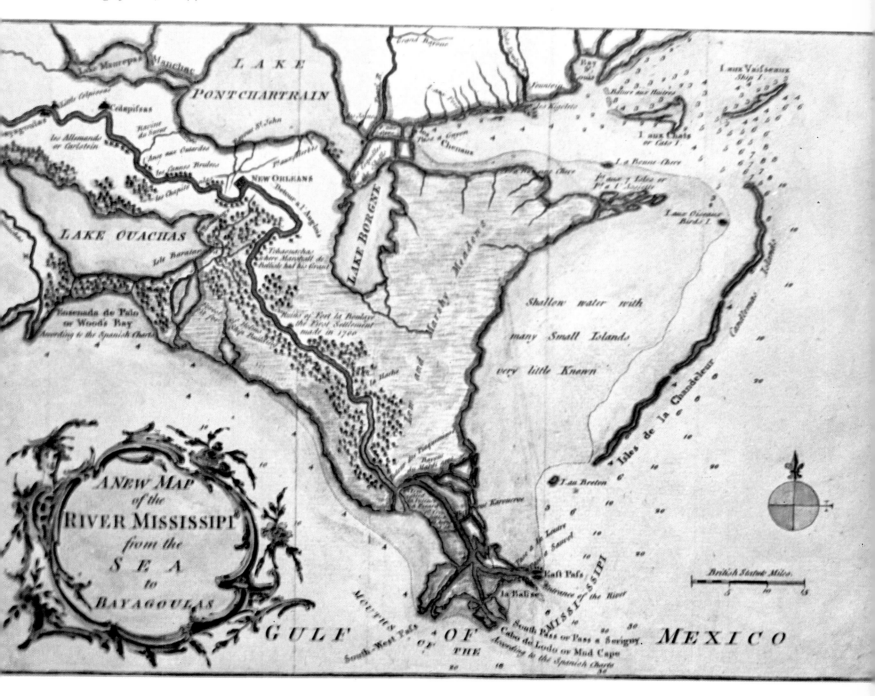

A NEW MAP
of the
RIVER MISSISSIPI
from the
SEA
to
BAYAGOULAS

Opposite: 'Carolina.' This map, by John Speed,
covers the whole of modern North and South
Carolina, with Cape Matteras in the foreground.
It is decorated with ships, Royal coats-of-
arms, and ships. Size of original 14¾ × 20 ins.
Published in 1676 by Bassett and Chiswell. (N)

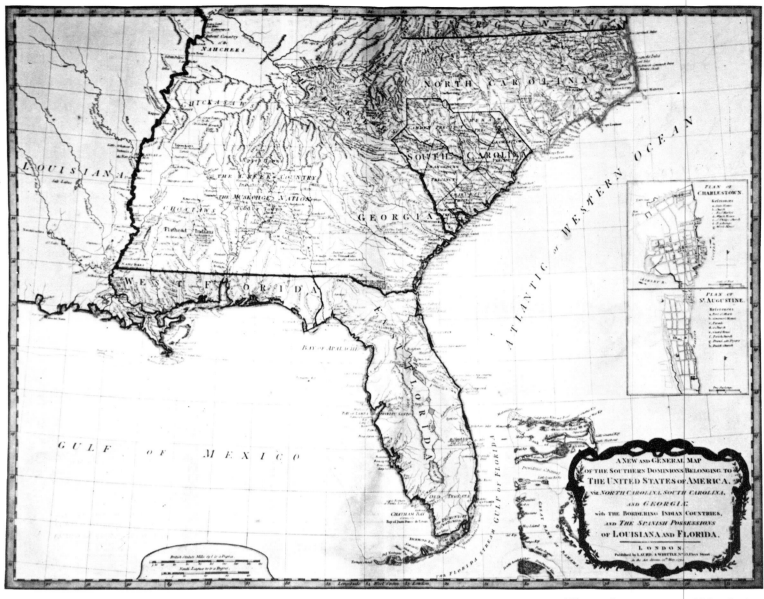

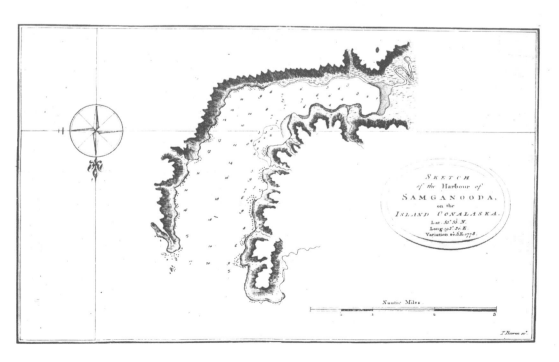

The south-eastern part of North America.
The map shows the southern states of the USA —
North and South Carolina and Georgia —
bordered to the west by the lands of the
Cherokees, Chicasaws, Creeks, Choctaws and
other Indian nations, and the then Spanish
possessions of Louisiana and Florida.
Published in London by Laurie and
Whittle in 1799. (N)

Opposite top: 'Massachusetts and Rhode Island.'
The inset shows Boston and its environs.
Size of original 12¾ × 15½ ins. Published by
J. H. Colton in 1859. (N)

Opposite: 'Canada, New Brunswick and
Nova Scotia.' Map of south-east Canada by
Sidney Hall. Size of original 16¾ × 20¾ ins.
Published by Longman, Pees, Orme, Brown
and Green in 1830. (CT)

'Sketch of the Harbour of Samganooda on the
Island Oonalaska.' Size of original 8 × 12¾ ins.
Engraved by T. Bowen. Published by Alex
Hogg c 1785. (CT)

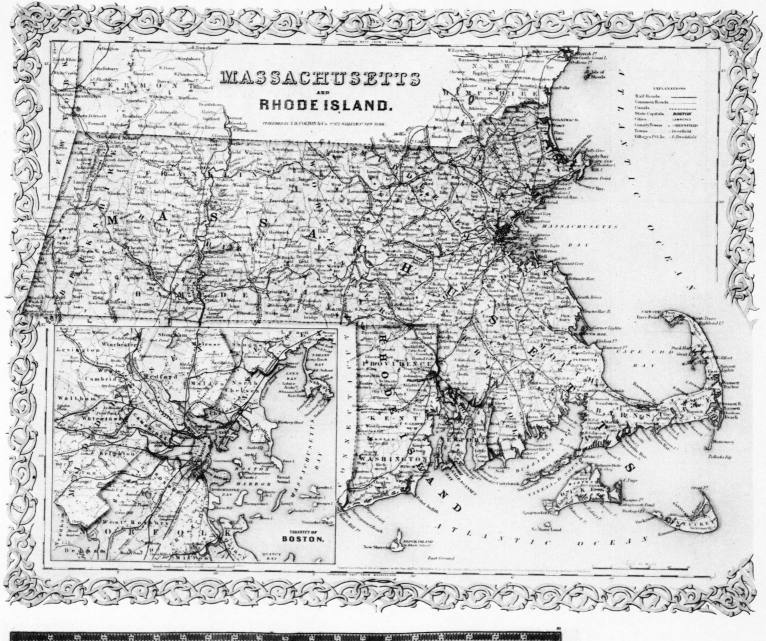

# MASSACHUSETTS
## AND
## RHODE ISLAND.

PUBLISHED BY J.H. COLTON & Co. N° 172 WILLIAM ST. NEW YORK.

VICINITY OF BOSTON.

## CANADA,
### NEW BRUNSWICK
### AND NOVA SCOTIA.

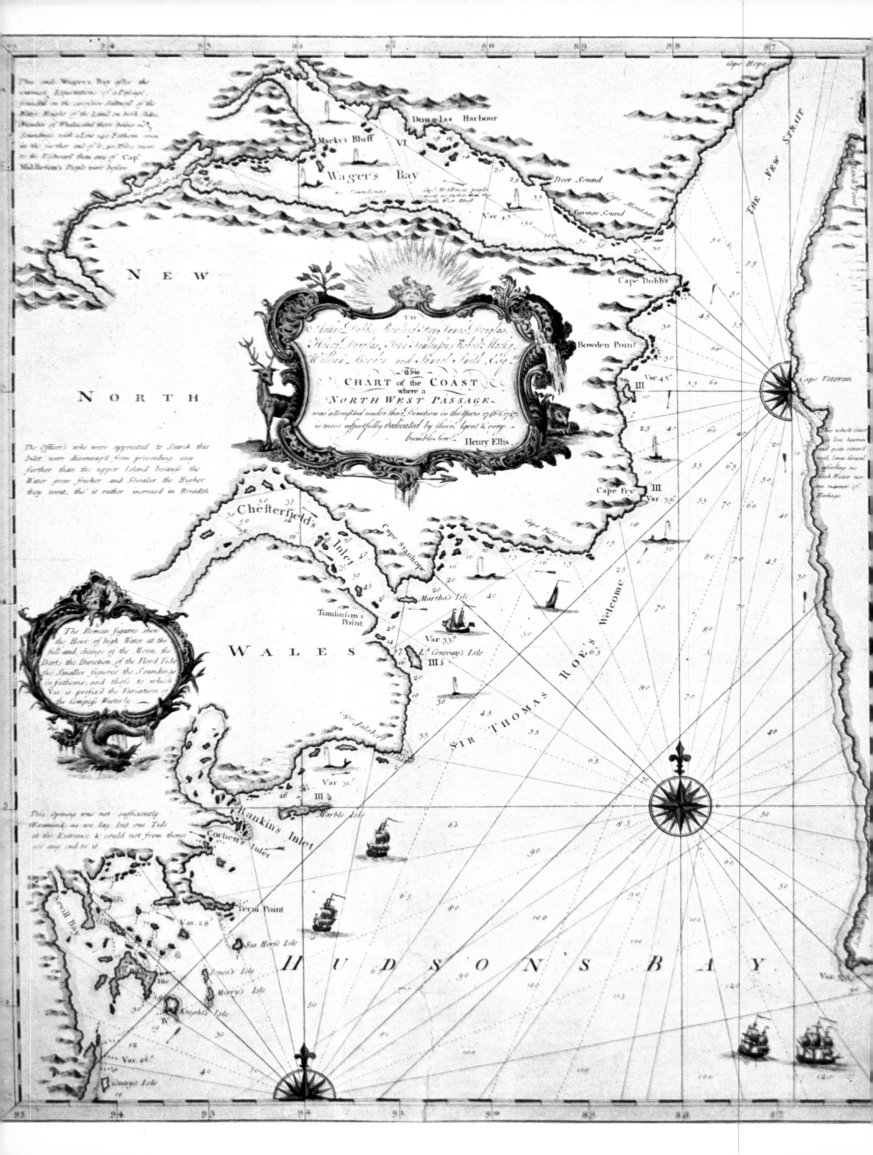

Left: *Hudson Bay. A chart of the coast,*
*decorated with cartouches, ships and whales.*
*Size of original 23¼ × 18½ ins.*
*Published in 1787 by R. Sayer.* (P)

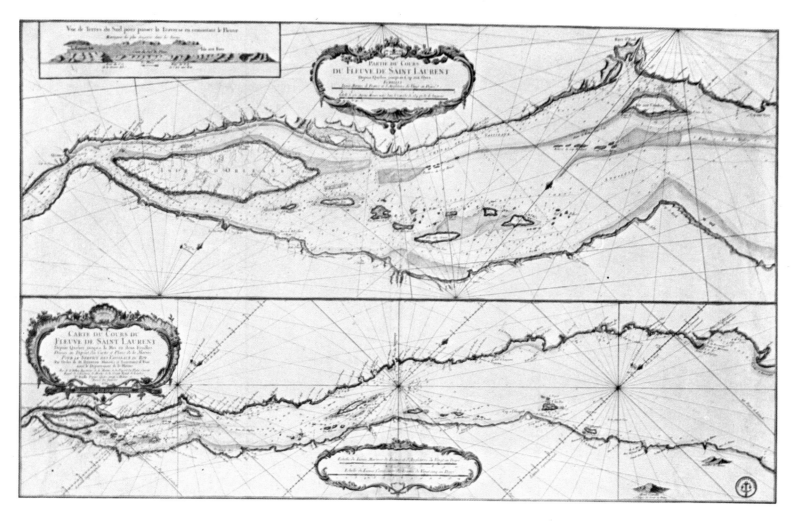

*Part of the course of the St Lawrence River*
*from Quebec to Cap aux Oyes (upper); map of*
*the course of the St Lawrence River from*
*Quebec to the sea (lower). A coloured chart*
*showing two charts on one sheet.*
*Size of original 22 × 33 ins. Published in*
*Paris in 1761 by J. Bellin.* (CT)

*South-eastern Canada. Map by Rigobert Bonne,*
*naval hydrographer, including Newfoundland*
*(la Terre Neuve), Nova Scotia (la Nouvelle*
*Ecosse) and Prince Edward Island (here known*
*as the Isle of St Jean). Size of original*
*8⅛ × 12⅜ ins. Published in 1780.* (N)

Opposite: 'East Canada and New Brunswick.' The map
shows the course of the St Lawrence from its
mouth to Beauharnois and is decorated with
drawings of Quebec and a group of North
American Indians. Map drawn and engraved by
J. Rapkin. Illustrations by H. Warren,
engraved by J. B. Allan. Size of original
10 × 13 ins. Published c 1850 by J. & E. Tallis. (CT)

Opposite, below: 'A New Map of Nova Scotia
and Cape Breton Island with the adjacent
parts of New England and Canada.'
Map by Thomas Jefferys. Size of original
18½ × 24 ins. Published in 1786. (N)

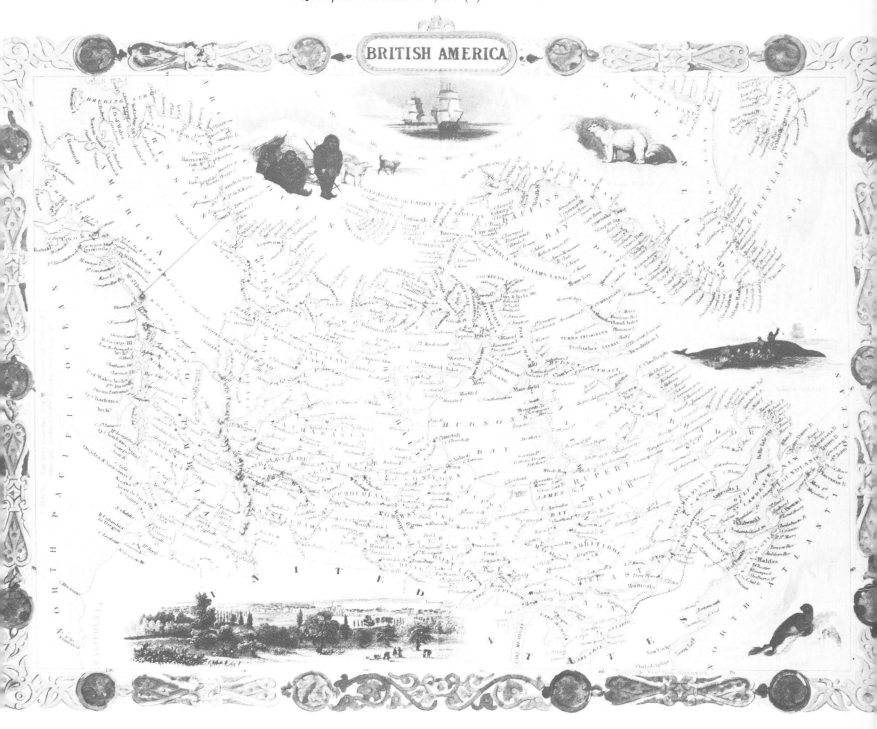

'British America.' Despite its title the map
also shows Russian America, Iceland and
Greenland. The drawings feature a view of
Montreal, Esquimaux, polar bears, whale
fishing, a seal and the ships Fury and Hecla.
Map drawn and engraved by J. Rapkin.
Illustrations by H. Warren, engraved by
R. Wallis. Size of original 10 × 12¾ ins.
Published by J. & E. Tallis c 1850. (CT)

# A COMPARATIVE VIEW OF THE PRINCIPAL WATERFALLS, ISLANDS, LAKES, RIVERS AND MOUNTAINS, IN THE WESTERN HEMISPHERE.

*'A comparative view of the principal Waterfalls,
Islands, Lakes, Rivers and Mountains in the
Western Hemisphere.' By John Rapkin.
Size of original 13 × 9½ ins. Published in 1850.* (CT)

*'A New Map of America.' Map by John
Senex decorated with a fine cartouche. Size of
original 19⅛ × 22¼ ins. Published in 1720.* (N)

‘South America.’ Map by Thomas Kitchen.
Size of original 7 × 9 ins. Published c 1765. (CT)

Above right: ‘Mexico, California and Texas.’
The drawings show a view of the ruins at Uxmal,
Yucatan; Mexican peasants and miners washing
gold. Size of original 10 × 13 ins. Map drawn
and engraved by J. Rapkin. Illustrations by
H. Warren, engraved by J. Rogers.
Published by J. Tallis in 1850. (CT)

Cartagena. A plan by J. Bellin of the town now
capital of the Bolivar department of Columbia.
Size of original 73⁄8 × 123⁄4 ins. Published c 1750. (CT)

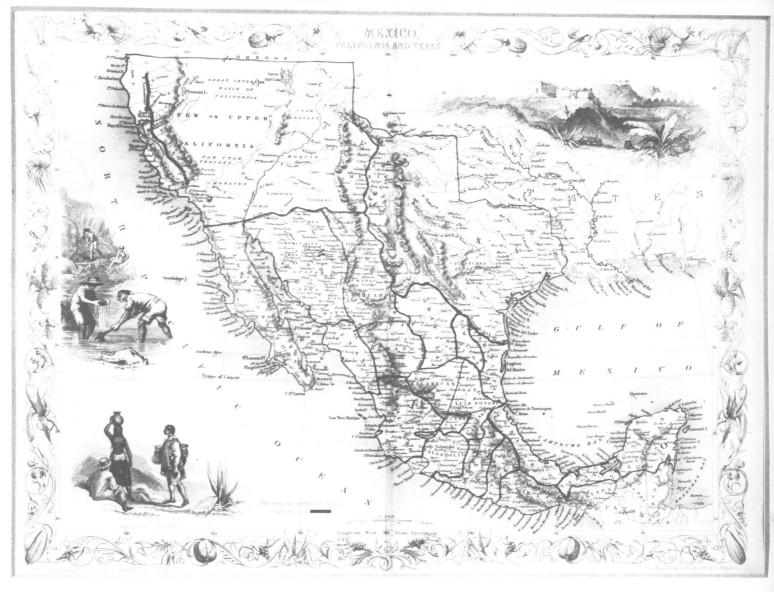

MEXICO, CALIFORNIA AND TEXAS

PLAN
DE LA VILLE DE
CARTHAGENE
des Indes

Situee par les 10 Deg. 25 Min 48 Sec de Lat.
Boreale et par les 301 Deg 19 Min de Longit.
comptee du Meridien de Teneriffe ou l'on voit
la Situation de cette Ville sur la Côte Nord
de l'Amerique Merid Levee par ordre du Roi
en 1735. Echelle de 200 Toises.

ISLE DE MANGA

A. Bastion de Ste Marie
B. Bastion de la Croix
C. Bastion de St Charles
D. Bastion de la Merced
E. Bastion de Ste Claire
F. Bast. de Ste Catherine
G. Bast. de St Luc
H. Bast. de St Philippe Martir
I. Bast. de St Jean
J. Bast. de St Vincent
K. Bast. de la Boucherie
L. Bast. du Pont
M. Bast. de St Ignace
N. Bast. de St Fr. Xavier
O. Bast. de St Jacques
P. Bast. Barahona St Phe.
Q. Bast. Ste Isabelle
R. Bast. St Laurens
S. Bast. St Joseph
T. Bast. de la demi Lune
V. Bast. de St Michel de Cambea
X. Fort de St Phil. de Barogas
Z. Hopital de St Lazare
1. Porte de la Contaderie
2. Porte du Pont
3. Porte de Ste Catherine
4. Porte St Domingue
5. Poterne de Mayco
6. Poterne de la Boucherie
7. Porte de la demi Lune
8. Poterne du Roi
9. Magasin a Poudre
10. Casernes
11. Prison
12. Ponts de communication
13. L'Eglise Cathedrale
14. Santo Domingo
15. St Augustin
16. St Juan de Dios
17. College des Jesuites
18. Eglise neuve des mêmes
19. la Merci
20. St Diego
21. Ste Clara ou Clairines
22. Ste Therese
23. St Francois
24. Parosse de la très Ste Trinate
25. Hermitage de St Roch
26. Maison ou l'on a fait les
Observations
27. la Tuerie
28. la Boucherie
29. St Toribio

'West Indies.' An old map by Thomas Jefferys decorated with a small cartouche showing a native labourer and overseers. Published in 1758. (CT)

Map of the Islands of St Domingue (Hispaniola) and Porto-rico. The map, by R. Bonne, a naval hydrographer, shows the larger island divided into a French part, corresponding roughly to modern Haiti, and a Spanish part, now the Dominican Republic. Size of original 8¼ × 12⅝ ins. Published in 1782. (CT)

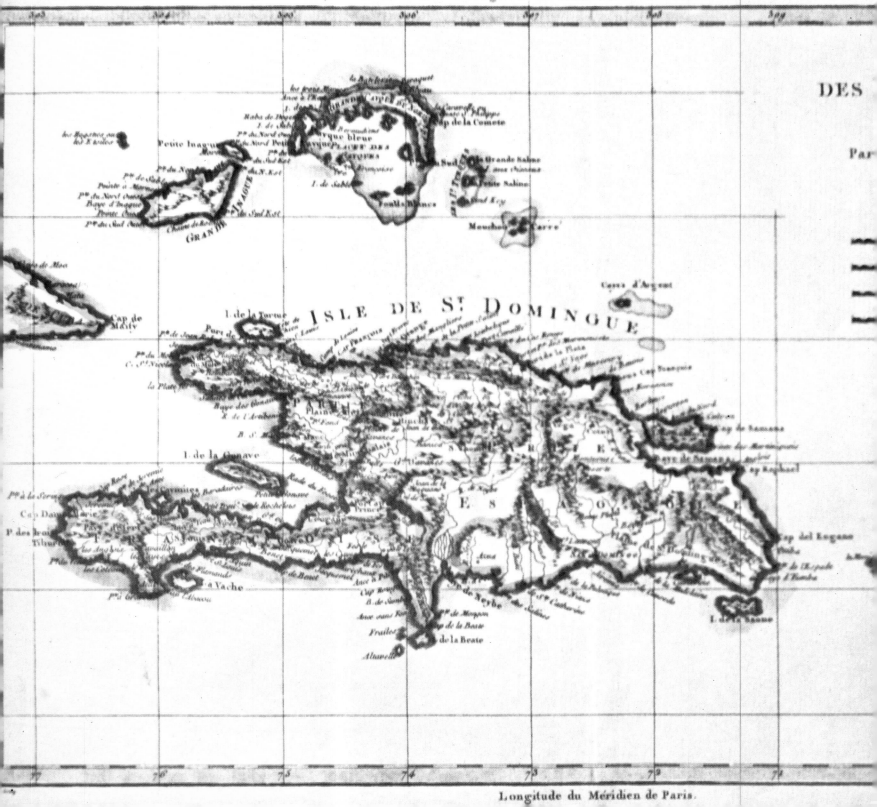

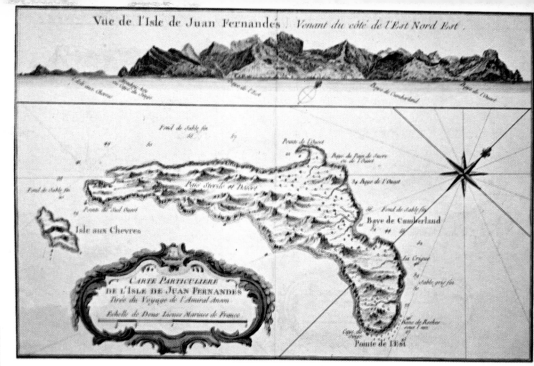

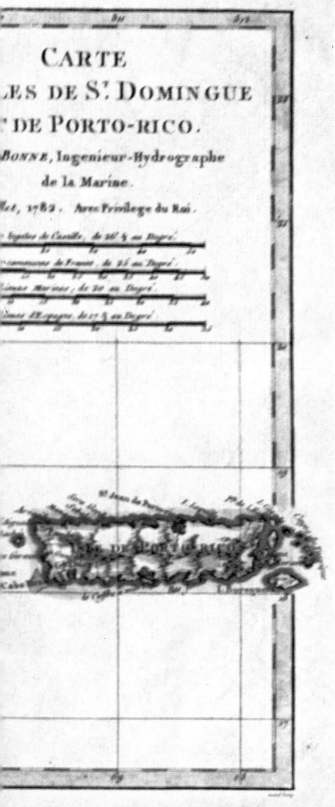

Individual Map of the Island of Juan
Fernandes. This map by J. Bellin, made
following the voyage of Admiral Anson, is
decorated with an attractive but simple scroll
cartouche, and a view of the island approached
from an east-north-easterly direction.
Size of original 7¾ × 11 ins. Published c 1754 (CT)

'Cape Verde Ilands.' A very simple miniature
map of this group of islands off the West
African coast, by Robert Morden. Size of
original 4½ × 5¼ ins. Published c 1680. (CT)

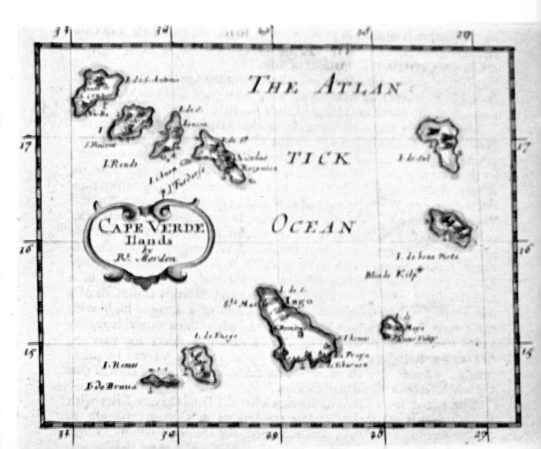

'*Abissina and Anian, etc.*' Map by Herman
Moll of some of the kingdom of north-east
Africa, with an inset of the strait now called
Bab-el-Mandeb (in Arabic 'Gate of Tears').
Size of original 7⅛ × 10⅛ ins.
Published in 1711. (CT)

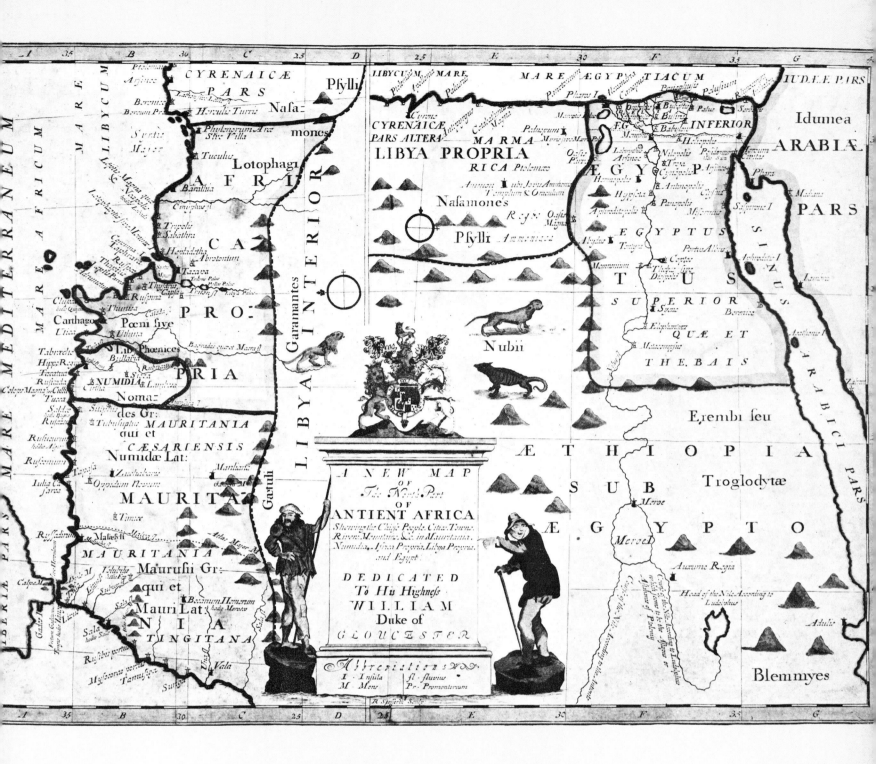

'The North Part of Antient Africa . . .
dedicated to His Highness William Duke of
Gloucester.' A very interesting old map by
Edward Wells with Royal Coat-of-Arms,
animals and figures. Size of original
14½ × 19¼ ins. Published in 1700. (N)

*'Nubia & Abissinia.' This map, by E. Bowen, also features the 'Kingdoms Tributary Thereto, and bordering upon them'. In area it roughly covers the land between Egypt, the Blue Nile and the Red Sea, extending in the south to the modern borders of Kenya and Somalia on the Indian Ocean. Size of original 13⅝ × 16¾ ins.* (CT)

A New and Accurate Map of
NUBIA & ABISSINIA,
together with all the
Kingdoms Tributary Thereto,
and bordering upon them,
Laid down from the
latest & best Authorities
and regulated by
Astron. Observations
By Eman. Bowen.

English Miles 60 to a Degree.
20 40 60 120 180 240 300

PART OF

THE RED SEA

ARABIA

Hadramut or
Schibam

Socotora I.

THE BUGIENS
Wandring People

SENNAR
NUBIA

KING OF TIGRA

K. OF
DANCALI

KINGDOM
OF
DAWARO

KINGD. OF BALLI

ADEL
OR OF
ZEILA

THE DESART COAST

GALLES
King of Ethiopia
GALLES

ETHIOPIA OR OF ABISSINIA

KINGD. OF
ALABA

K. OF
MACHIDA

A J A N

Nation of Dadas

The Arbores or Afhbores

The Arvisas

The Brefomas

KINGDOM OF
MAGADOXA

The Maracates Mohamedans
who possess this Country till within
about two Days Journey of the Sea

The Equinoctial Line

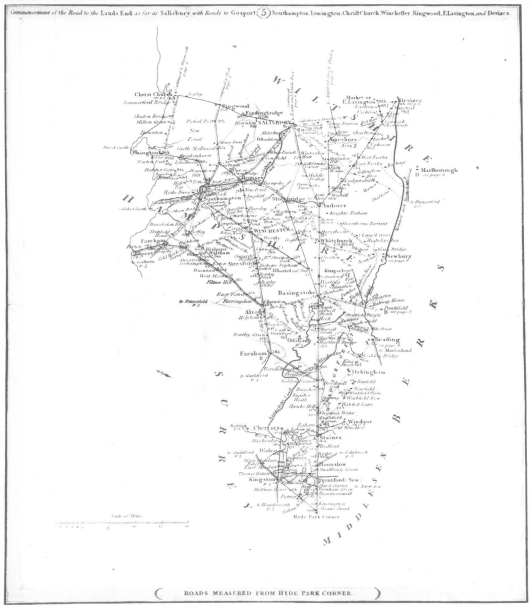

ROADS MEASURED FROM HYDE PARK CORNER.

*The Road from Hyde Park Corner to Salisbury,*
*etc. One of a series of road maps showing the*
*route from Hyde Park Corner to Land's End.*
*Size of original 12 × 9¾ ins. Published by*
*Laurie and Whittle* c 1808. (CT)

'Herefordshire.' County map by Robert Morden.
*Size of original 14 × 16½ ins. Published in 1695.* (CT)

'The Invasions of England and Ireland with al their Civill Wars since the Conquest.' A very rare map, by John Speed, showing battles in progress on land and sea, with short descriptions of each. Size of original 15 × 20¼ ins. Engraved by C. Danckerts. Published in 1676 by Bassett and Chiswell. (N)

'Glamorganshire.' A small county map by John Seller. Original size 4¼ × 5¾ ins. Published in 1701. (N)

'Somersetshire.' A county map by John Speed
showing inset plan of the City of Bath,
the Royal Arms, ships, and coats-of-arms
of important county families. Size of
original 14⅝ × 19½ ins. Published by
Sudbury and Humble c 1614. (N)

Right: Bedfordshire. An antique coloured map of the
county by J. Blaeu, decorated with coat-of-arms
associated with the Dukes of Bedford. Size of
original 16½ × 9½ ins. Published c 1660. (CT)

Cumberland. Detail of cartouche on the map of
Cumberland by Joan Blaeu (1648). The scroll
work represents wood-carving typical of the
period. The figures and birds provide a well-
balanced pastoral scene. (CT)

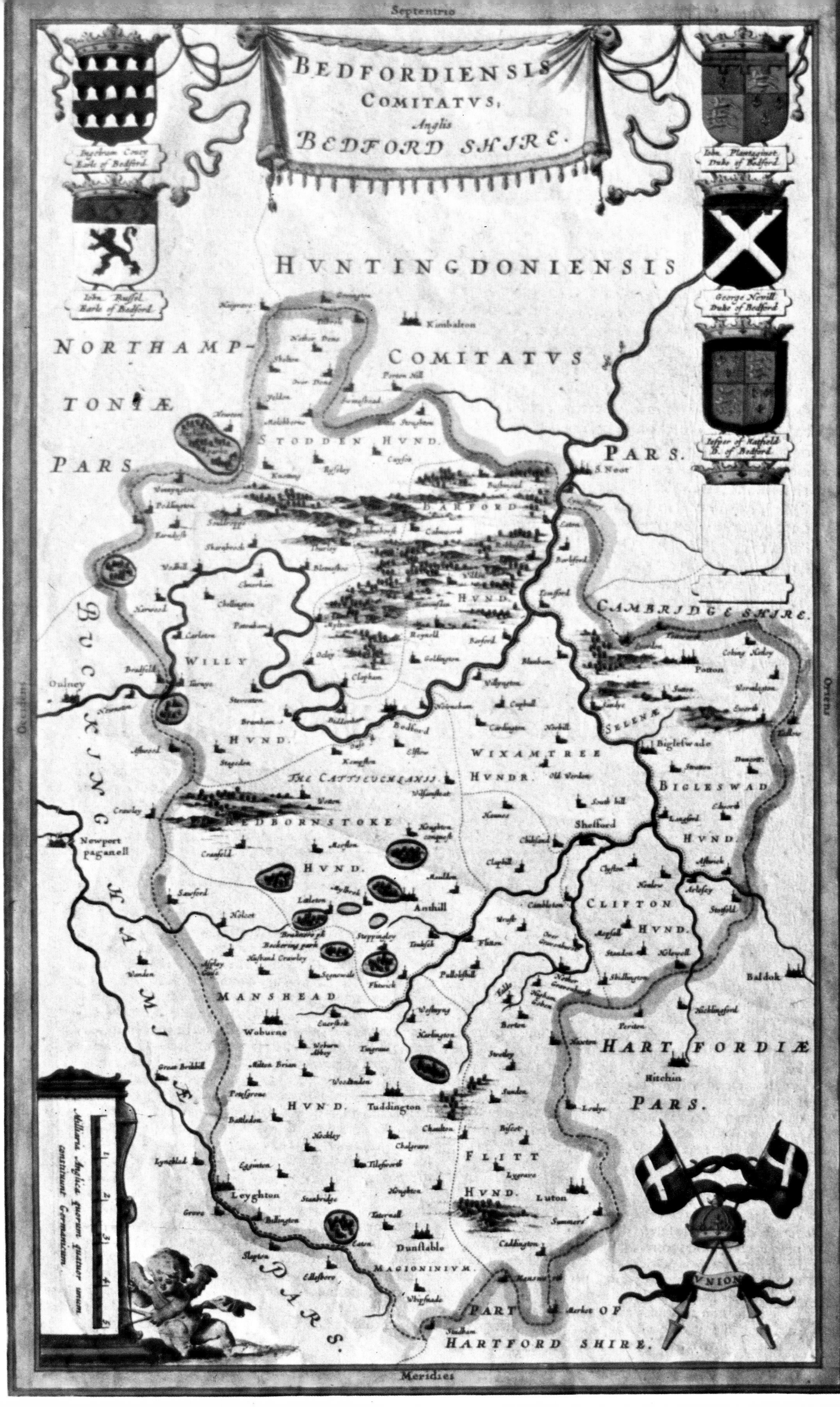

# BEDFORDIENSIS COMITATVS, Anglis BEDFORD SHIRE.

Septentrio

Meridies

Occidens

Oriens

HVNTINGDONIENSIS COMITATVS PARS.

NORTHAMP-TONIÆ PARS.

BUCKINGHAMIÆ PARS.

CAMBRIDGESHIRE.

HARTFORDIÆ PARS.

STODDEN HVND.

BARFORD

WILLY HVND.

WIXAMTREE HVNDR.

BIGLESWAD HVND.

CLIFTON HVND.

REDBORNSTOKE HVND.

MANSHEAD HVND.

FLITT HVND.

THE CATTIEUCHLANIS

SELENA

Kimbalton

S. Neot

Bedford

Biglesswade

Potton

Baldok

Newport paganell

Oulney

Woburne

Woburn Abbey

Tuddington

Leyghton

Dunstable

Luton

Hitchin

Leedye

MAGIONINIVM.

UNION

PART OF HARTFORD SHIRE.

Kent. County map by Owen/Bowen. The rather
heavy decorative cartouche on the top indicates
main routes covered on the map. Size of original
7 ×4½ ins. Published c 1720. (N)

Sussex. A companion to the previous map,
by Owen/Bowen. Size of original 7 ×4½ ins.
Published c 1720. (N)

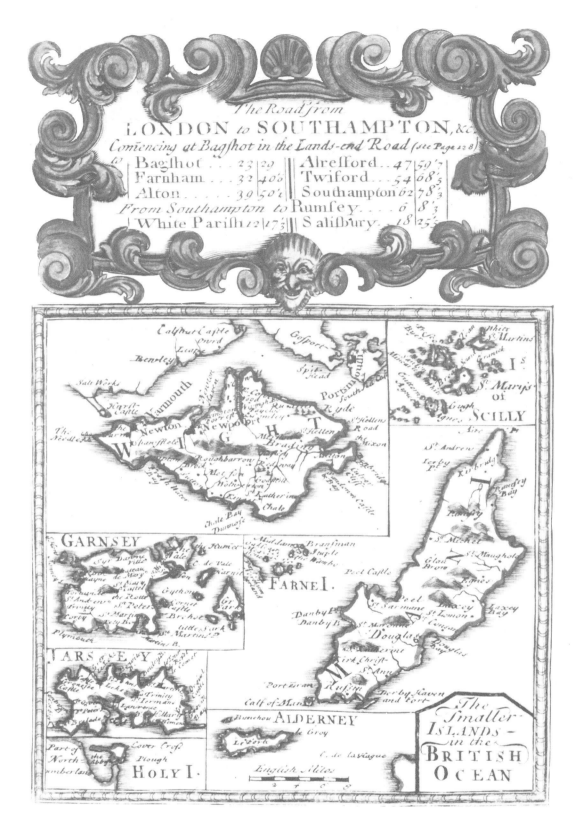

'The Smaller Islands in the British Oceans.'
Separate plans of the Isles of Wight, Scilly,
'Garnsey', 'Jarsey', Man, Farne, Holy Island
and Alderney. Size of original 7 × 4½ ins.
By Owen/Bowen. Published c 1720. (N)

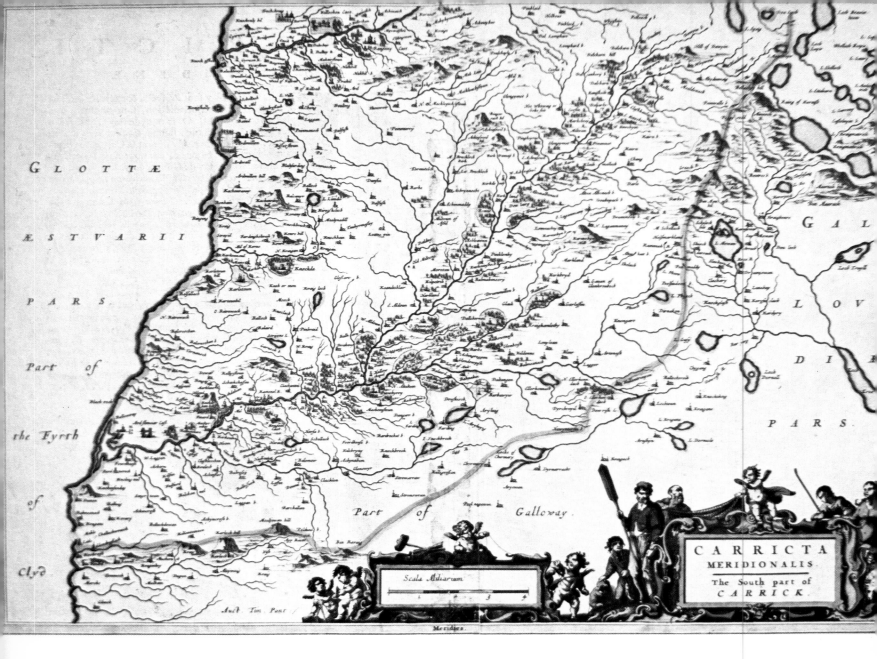

'Carricta Meridionalis – The South part of
Carrick.' To the west of this region of Ayrshire
is the Firth of Clyde, to the east is part of
Galloway. The map, by J. Blaeu, was engraved
by Timothy Pont. Size of original 15 × 21 ½ ins.
Published c 1646. (CT)

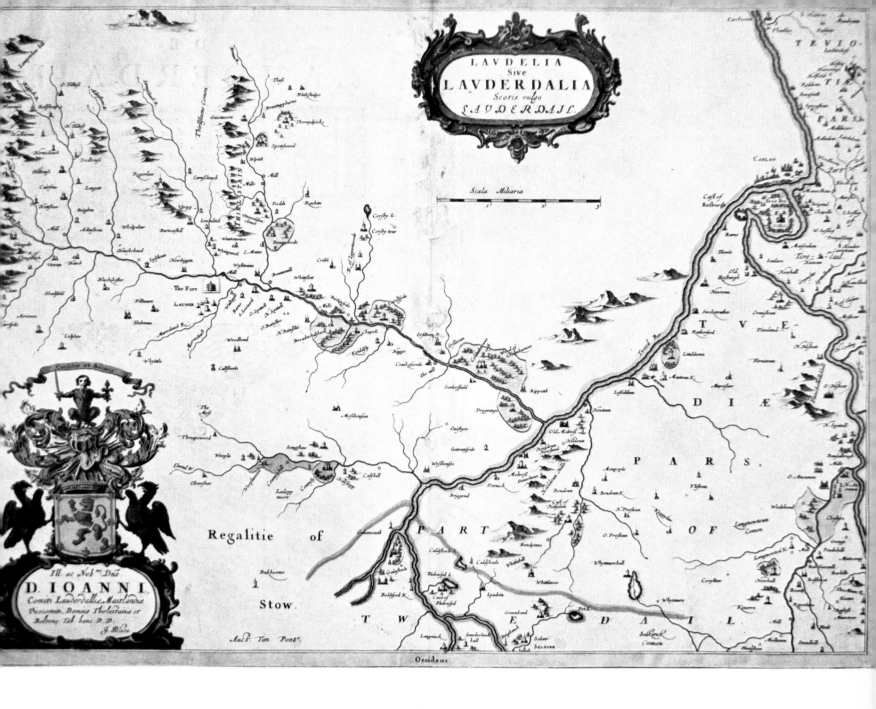

'Laudelia Sive Lauderdalia.' Beautiful coloured map by J. Blaeu, decorated with an elaborate cartouche, showing the Tweed River mainly in the modern county of Roxburghshire. Size of original 15¼ × 20 ins. Engraved by Timothy Pont. Published c 1645. (CT)

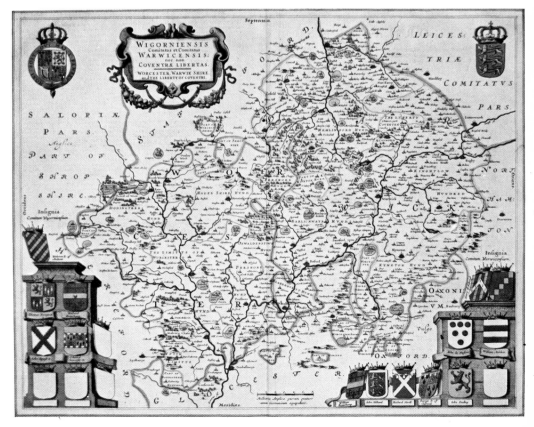

'Worcester, Warwikshire and The Liberty of Coventre.' Coloured two-county map by J. Blaeu, decorated with coats-of-arms. French text on back. Size of original 16⅛ × 19⅝ ins. Published c 1648. (N)

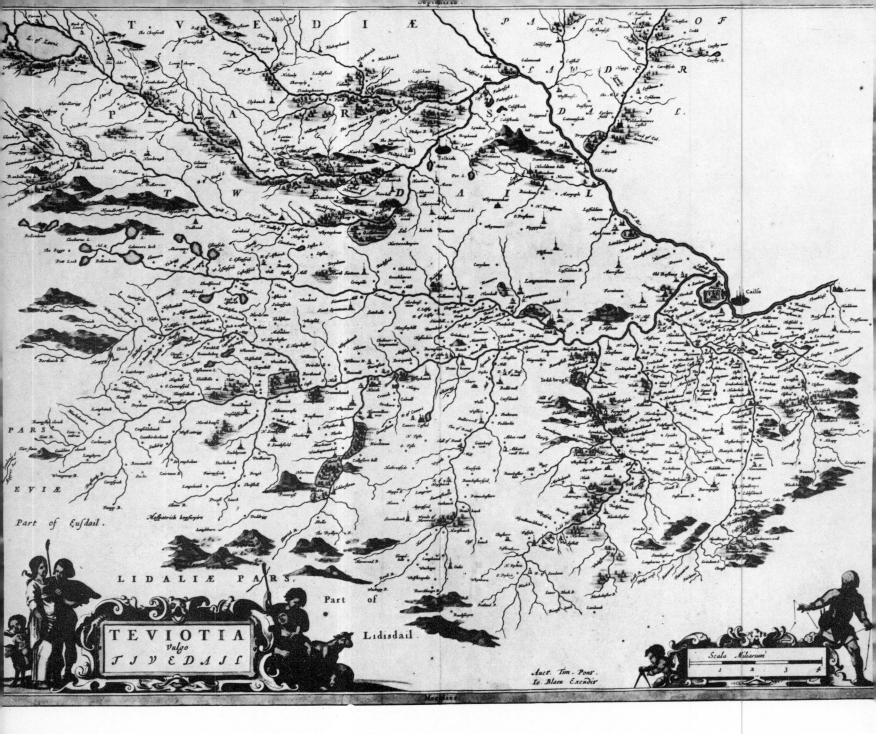

'Teviotia.' A map of Teviotdale, Scotland,
by Joan Blaeu. Size of original 16¾ × 20¾ ins.
Published in 1654. (N)

Opposite, top: 'The Isle of Man.' Map by Thomas
Moule with decorative border. Size of original
7¾ × 10½ ins. Published by G. Virtue c 1833. (N)

Opposite: 'A New Map of the British Isles.'
The map, by S. Nicholls, shows 'their Present
Genl. Divisions, Cities, and such other Towns,
or Places, as answer to the Towns of Note
in the time of the Romans'. It is dedicated to
William, Duke of Gloucester. Size of original
14⅝ × 19½ ins. Published c 1700. (CT)

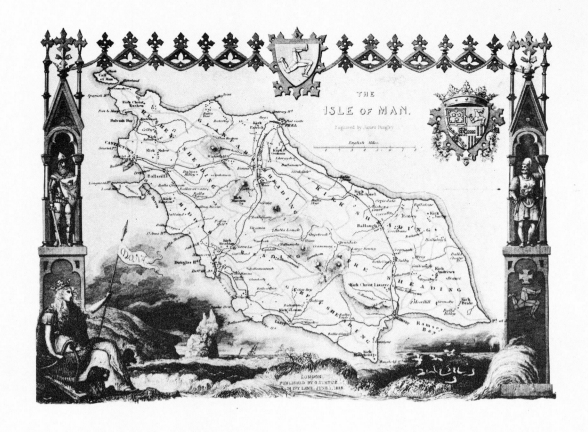

THE
ISLE OF MAN.

Engraved by James Bingley

English Miles

LONDON
PUBLISHED BY G. VIRTUE
26 IVY LANE, JUNE 1, 1833.

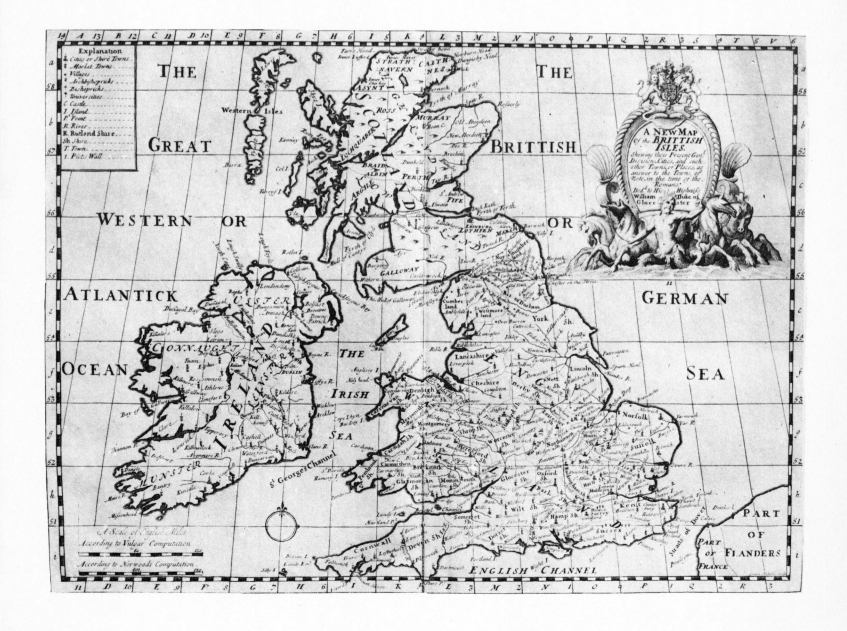

Explanation
Cities or Shire Towns
Market Towns
Villages
Archbishopricks
Bishopricks
Universities
C. Castle
I. Island
F. Point
R. River
R. Rutland Shire
Sh. Shire
T. Town
1. Picts Wall

A NEW MAP
of the
BRITTISH
ISLES.
Shewing their Present Gen.l
Divisions, Cities, and such
other Towns, or Places, as
answer to the Towns, of
Note, in the time of the
Romans:
Ded.d to His Highness
William Duke of
Gloucester

THE GREAT WESTERN OR ATLANTICK OCEAN

THE BRITTISH OR GERMAN SEA

IRELAND

ULSTER
CONNAUGHT
LEINSTER
MUNSTER

THE IRISH SEA

St. Georges Channel

ENGLISH CHANNEL

PART OF FLANDERS
PART OF FRANCE

A Scale of English Miles
According to Vulgar Computation
According to Norwoods Computation

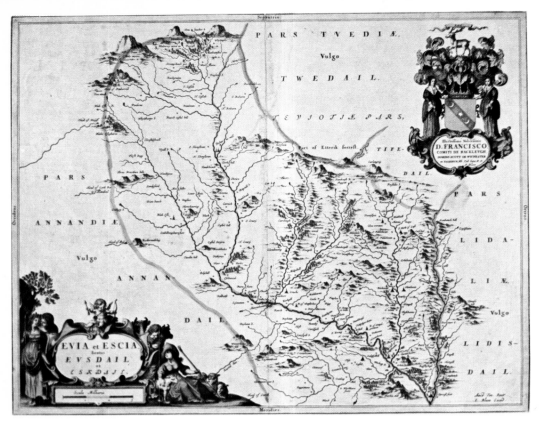

'*Evia et Escia.*' *Another of J. Blaeu's Scottish series showing the Eskdale district of Dumfriessshire. The elaborate cartouche depicts rural life with a shepherdess, a cowherd and other figures. Size of original 16½ × 20⅝ ins. Engraved by Timothy Pont.* (CT)

*Details showing the cartouches on the Eskdale map by J. Blaeu.* (CT)

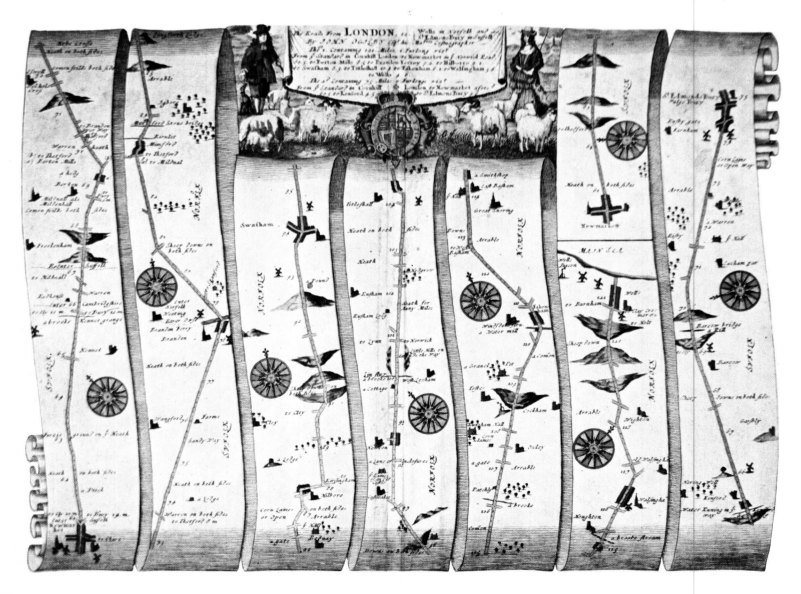

'The Countie of Leinster.' Antique coloured
map of the county by Jan Jansson.
Size of original 15 × 19¼ ins.
Published in Amsterdam c 1660. (P)

Opposite: 'The Roads from London to Wells
in Norfolk and St Edmons Bury (Bury St
Edmunds) in Suffolk.' A strip map by John Ogilby
showing the recommended routes with landmarks
indicated. Note the reversed hills to indicate
that the traveller is proceeding downhill.
Size of original 12¾ × 17 ins. Published c 1670. (CT)

Staffordshire. Antique coloured map of the
county by J. Blaeu, decorated with rural
cartouches and coats-of-arms. Size of original
16 × 15⅝ ins. Published c 1648. (N)

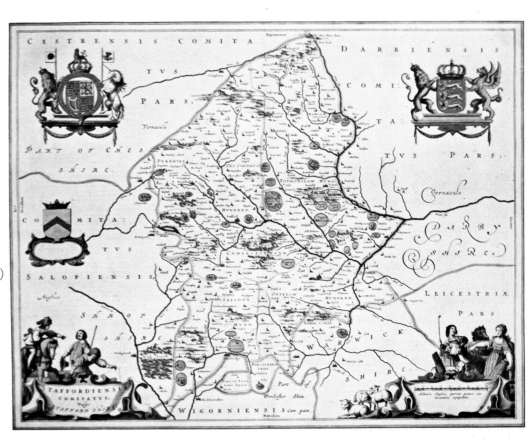

*'England.' Map of England (and Wales) by Robert Morden. Size of original 14⅛ × 16⅜ ins. Published c 1700. (AUTHOR'S COLLECTION)*

*Scottish Road Map. The map starts at Inverness and traces two routes, one to Fort Augustus and Fort William, the other to Glen Urquhart, on the opposite side of Loch Ness. Size of original 18¼ × 7¼ ins. Published by Taylor and Skinner in 1776.* (N)

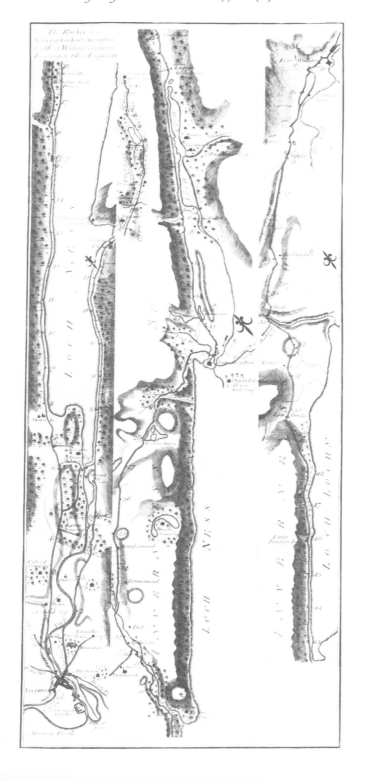

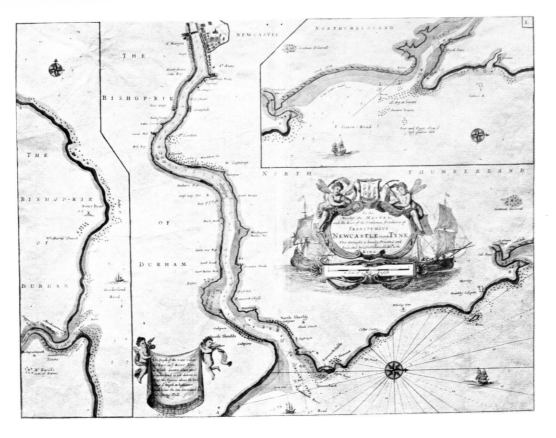

'Newcastle uppon Tyne.' A beautiful chart by Captain Grenville Collins, dedicated to 'the Master and the Rest of the Gentlemen Bretheren of Trinity Hous'. The cartouche is particularly decorative with scrolls, cherubs and ships. Size of original 17¼ × 21¾ ins. Engraved by H. Moll. Published in 1693. (CT)

Opposite: Dorsetshire. A decorative map of the county by C. Saxton ornamented with Royal Arms, ships and a sea monster. Size of original 10¾ × 15 ins. Engraved by W. Kip. Published in 1637. (CT)

Below: 'Penbrokshyre.' An attractive coloured map of this Welsh county by John Speed with inset plans of Pembroke and St David's. Decorated with an ornamental cartouche surmounted with the Royal Coat-of-Arms and eleven other coats-of-arms. Size of original approx. 20 × 16 ins. Published c 1676. (CT)

Opposite, below: 'Chester.' A county map by H. Moll, decorated on the end border with altars and two Roman brooches (fibulas). Size of original 7½ × 10 ins. Published in 1724.

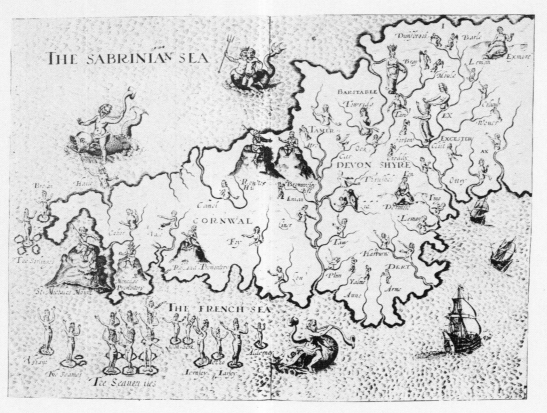

Cornwall and Devonshire. An unusual map by Michael Drayton showing water-nymphs bathing in the rivers, many of which are being created or sustained by the activities of water-powers; other figures, shepherds, etc., appear on the hills and elsewhere. Neptune is shown with another figure, there are giant fish, and a few ships occupy the bay. The Venus-like figures represent islands as far afield as Ushant and the Channel Isles. The map was published in 1612 for the 'Polyolbion', a poetic work by Drayton. (N)

'A New and Correct Chart of the Channel between England and France.' An eighteenth-century chart with inset plans of Plymouth Sound and the Isle of Wight.
Size of original 25 × 39½ ins.
Published by Page & Mount in 1729. (CT)

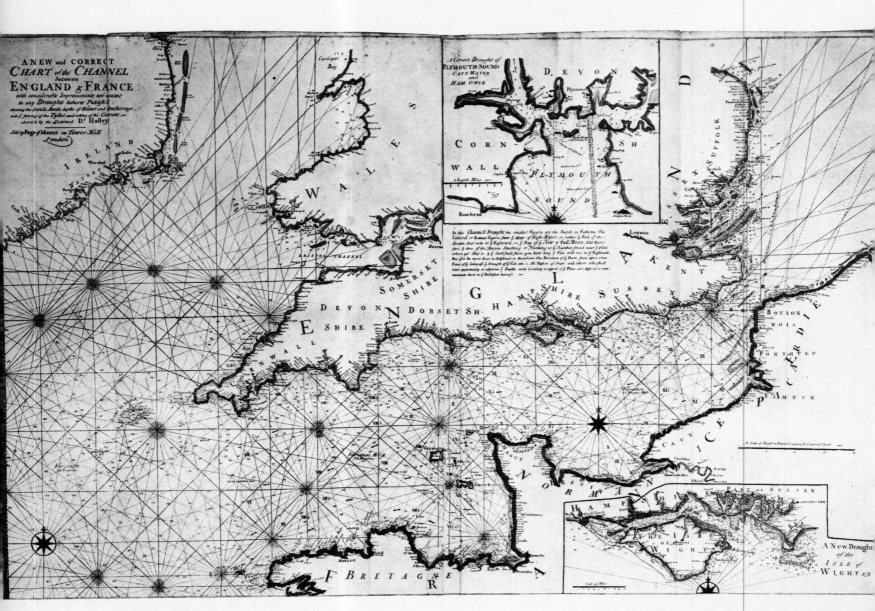

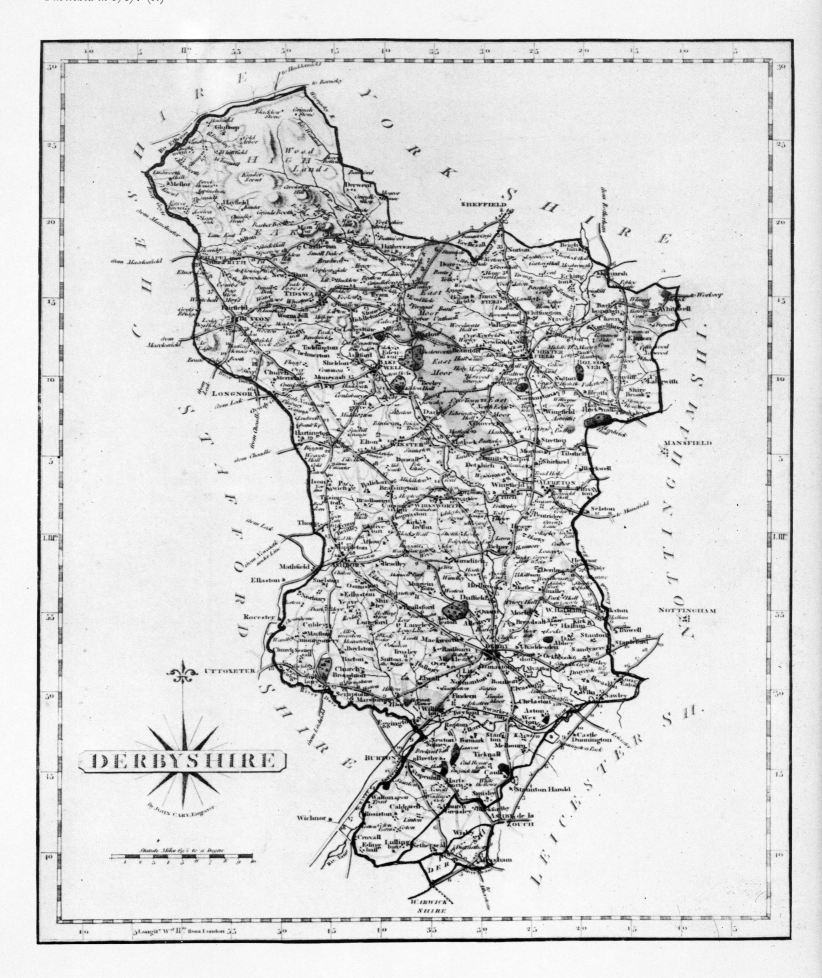

*'Derbyshire.' County map by John Cary.*
*Size of original 10⅜ × 8¼ ins.*
*Published in 1787.* (N)

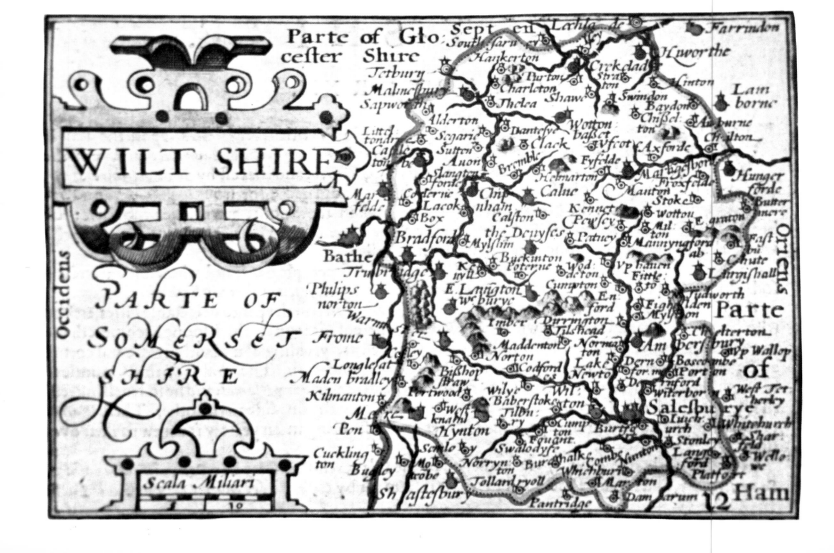

Opposite: 'Sussex.' A miniature map of the
county by van den Keere. The back of the
map has a descriptive text in English.
Size 3¼ × 4¾ ins. Published in 1627.

Opposite, below: 'Wiltshire.' A miniature map
of the county by van den Keere. The back of the
map has a descriptive text in English.
Size of original 3⅜ × 4¾ ins.
Published in 1627. (N)

'Hantshire.' A fine antique coloured map by
John Speed of Hampshire, decorated with
coats-of-arms, an inset plan of Winchester and
a picture of the Empress Maud escaping
from Winchester in a coffin. Size of original
14⅞ × 20 ins. Engraved by J. Hondius.
Published in 1614 by Sudbury and Humble. (N)

‘Glasgow.’ A plan of the city by J. Rapkin
with inset views of the University, Royal Bank
of Scotland, Glasgow seen from the Green,
the Cathedral, the Royal Exchange and
New Bridge. Illustrations drawn and engraved by
H. Winkles. Size of original 14 × 19 ins.
Published by John Tallis in 1850. (N)

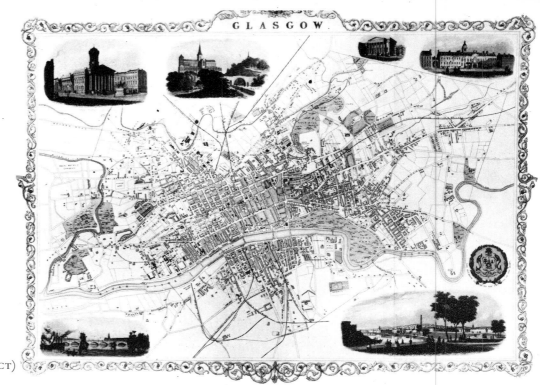

‘Cornwall.’ Another county map by E. Bowen
showing Cornwall ‘Divided into its Hundreds
Containing all the Buroughs & Market,
Towns with the Roads & Distances &c.’
The Isles of Scilly are promised in some future
part of the work ‘together with other Islands’.
Size of original 7 × 7¾ ins. Published c 1756. (CT)

'Kent.' In this map by E. Bowen the county is
'Divided into its Lathes (administrative areas)
Containing the Cities, Burough and Market
Towns'. Size of original 6¾ × 7¾ ins.
The legend at the foot explains that the map was
'Engraved for the General Magazine of Arts
and Sciences for W. Owen at Temple Bar 1756'. (CT)

The British Isles. Map by Nicolas Sanson with
inset plan of the Shetland Isles. Size of original
15¾ × 20¾ ins. Published in 1658. (N)

*Norfolk. A county map by John Speed and C. Saxton. The picture on the left is a representation of a medieval battle and the text gives short accounts of local rebellious deeds by John Litistar and Robert Kett. Kett led a revolt against land enclosures: in 1549 he stormed Norwich but was defeated and executed. Size of original 14¼ × 19½ ins. Engraved by F. Goddard and published by Thomas Bassett and Richard Chiswell in 1676.* (CT)

*Buckinghamshire. A county map by John Speed decorated with coats-of-arms and inset plans of Buckingham and Reading – the latter being included here because, as the artist explains: 'For that Barkshire cold not contayn place for this Towne I have here inserted it . . .' Size of original 15 × 20 ins. Published 1676 by Bassett and Chiswell.* (N)

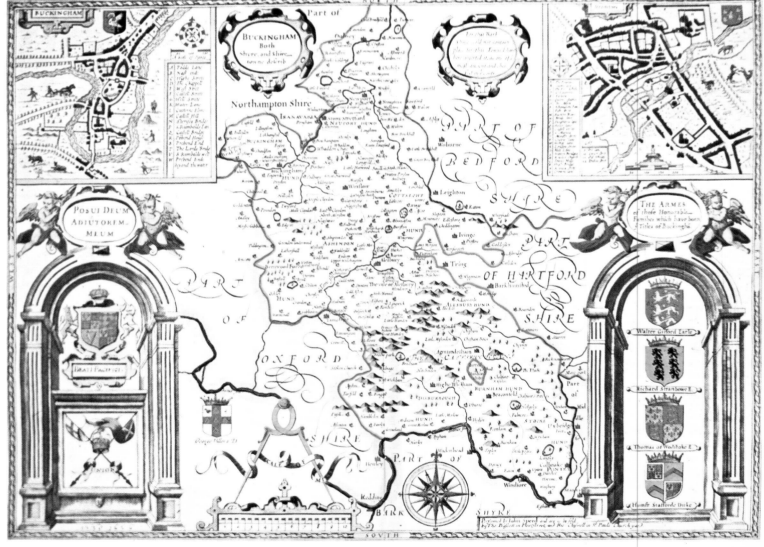

'Wales.' A John Speed map decorated with surrounding inset plans of 'Beaumaris (in Anglesey), Bangor, Carnarvon, Harlieg, Cardigan, Penbrok, Carmarthen, St David's, Landafe, Cardife, Brecknok (Brecon), Radnor, Montgomery, Flint, Denbigh, St Asaph'. Other decorations include coats-of-arms, ships and sea monsters. Size of original 15 × 20 ins. Published by John Sudbury and Geo. Humble c 1628. (P)

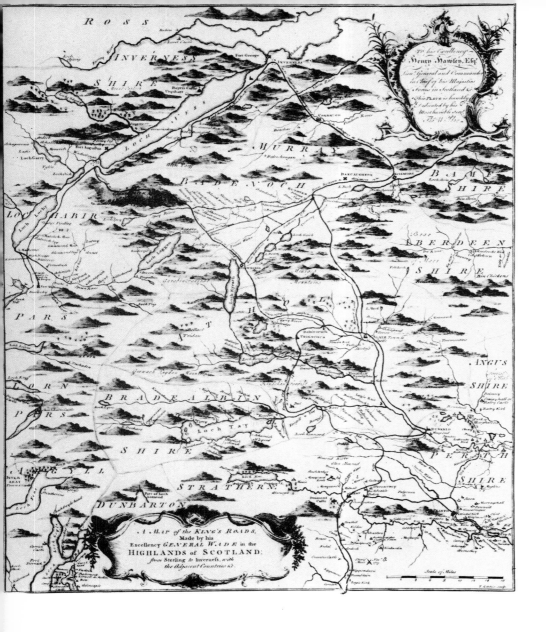

'*A Map of the King's Roads Made by his Excellency General Wade in the Highlands of Scotland from Sterling to Inverness.*' Size of original 18 × 15 ins. Published by Thomas Willdey in 1746. (N)

Opposite: '*Northamptonshire.*' County map by Thomas Moule with inset views of Althorpe House, Northampton, Queen's Cross and Peterborough Cathedral. Size of original 10¼ × 7½ ins. Published c 1840. (N)

'*A Mapp of Devonshire.*' This county map illustrates the untidy engraving typical of Richard Blome. Size of original 10 × 12¼ ins. Published in 1673. (CT)

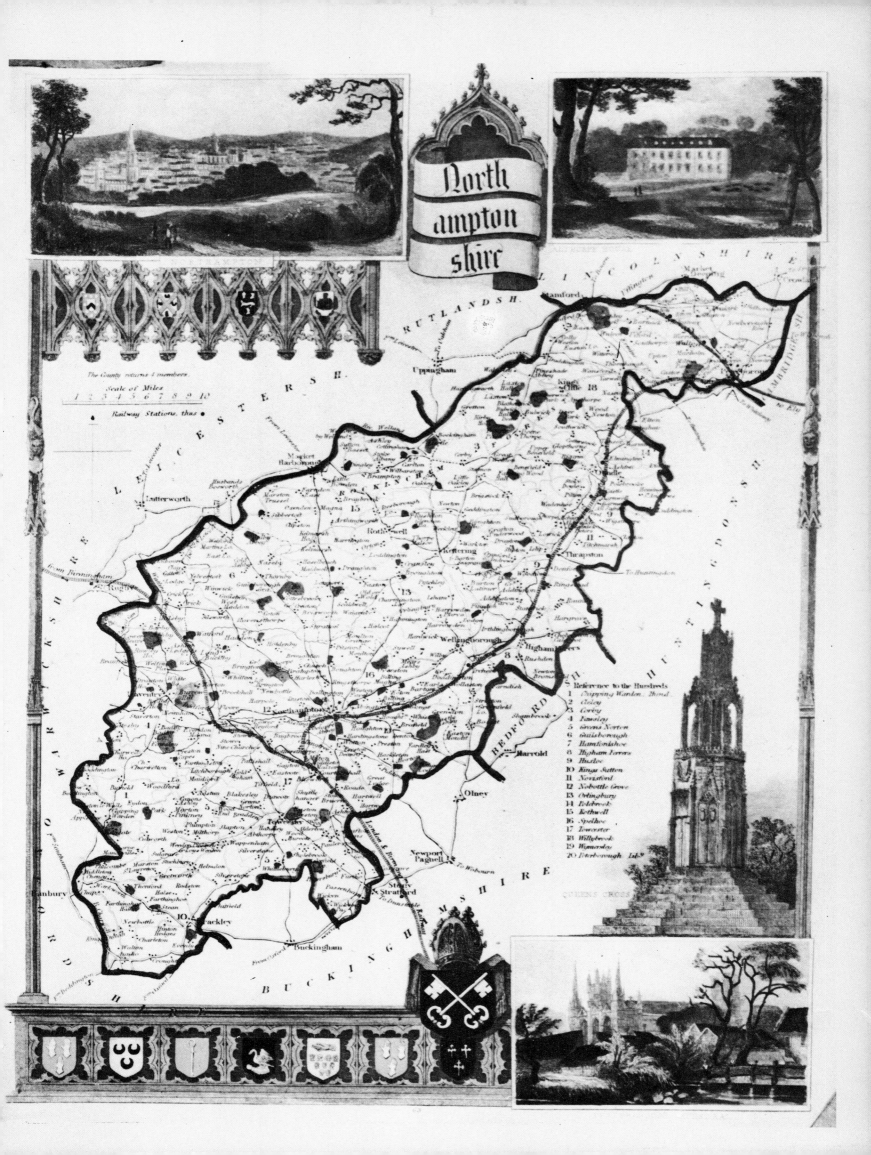

# North ampton shire

LINCOLNSHIRE

RUTLANDSH.

LEICESTERSH.

WARWICKSHIRE

CAMBRIDGESH.

HUNTINGDONSH.

BEDFORD SH.

BUCKINGHAMSHIRE

OXFORD SH.

The County returns 4 members.

Scale of Miles
1 2 3 4 5 6 7 8 9 10

Railway Stations, thus •

**Reference to the Hundreds**
1 Chipping Warden Thond.
2 Cleley
3 Corby
4 Fausley
5 Greens Norton
6 Guilsborough
7 Hamfordshoe
8 Higham Ferers
9 Huxloe
10 Kings Sutton
11 Newsford
12 Nobottle Grove
13 Ordingbury
14 Polebrook
15 Rothwell
16 Spelhoe
17 Towcester
18 Willybrook
19 Wimersley
20 Peterborough Lib.y

QUEENS CROSS

Uppingham
Stamford
Market Harborough
Lutterworth
Rugby
From Birmingham
Daventry
Naseby
Rothwell
Kettering
Oundle
Thrapston
To Huntingdon
Wellingborough
Higham Ferrers
Rushden
Northampton
Towcester
Harrold
Olney
Newport Pagnell
Stony Stratford
Buckingham
To Dunstable Railway
Banbury
Brackley

Opposite, top: *'The Upper Ward of Clyds-dayl. Map of Clydesdale, Lanarkshire, by J. Blaeu, engraved by Timothy Pont. Size of original 15¼ × 20¾ ins. Published c 1646.* (CT)

Bottom right: *'Orkney.' The map shows the chief harbours in the Islands of Orkney, and is dedicated to Captain Will Bond by Captain Grenville Collins, Royal Hydrographer. Size of original 17⅜ × 21¾ ins.* (CT)

*Hertfordshire. Coloured map by C. Saxton decorated with large cartouche surmounted by Royal Coat-of-arms. Size of original 15⅝ × 19⅝ ins. Published in 1577.* (N)

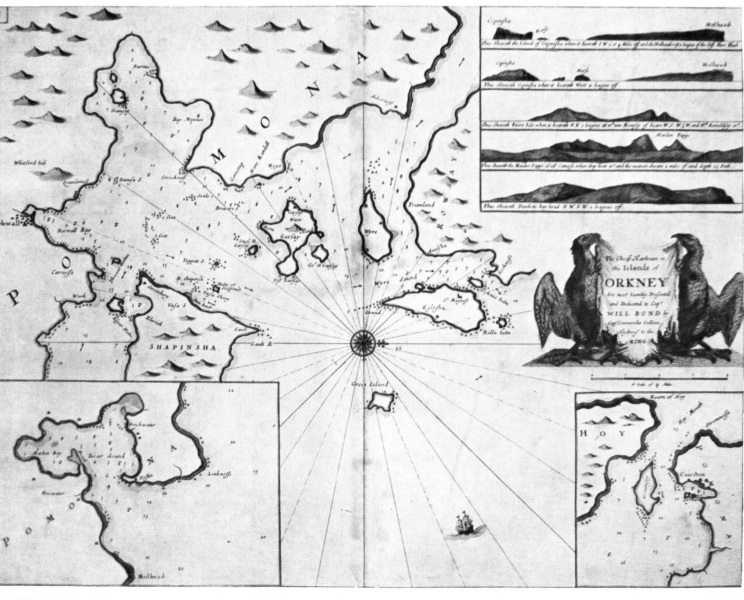

# Index